I0473400

# RASCHE NOTATION
## Dance Notation for Argentine Tango

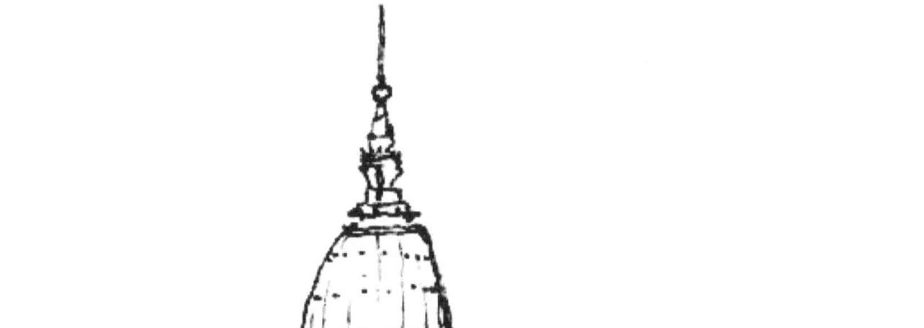

## by Thomas Rasche

**Rasche Notation**
**Dance Notation for Argentine Tango**

Author: Thomas Rasche

ISBN 978-0-9561489-0-2

First published in March 2009
Published by Thomas Rasche

Print and distribution by Lulu.com

Thomas Rasche, Suite 105, 179 Whiteladies Road, Clifton, Bristol BS8 2AG, UK. Email: thomas@RascheNotation.com, Web: www.RascheNotation.com

If you would like to publish your own notation on the web, you can add this logo to your web page(s) as a link to the Rasche Notation homepage at Rasche.Notation.com. This will help other people find out more information:

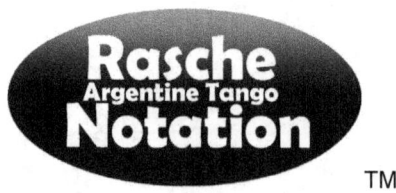

TM

Review of Rasche Notation:
"The author has dared to challenge this race towards the madness [of writing all the nuances] and endeavoured to find a way to write down the dance of tango; with astonishment and happiness I can say that he has achieve it well."
Damián Esell, Buenos Aires, 2007. Review of Rasche Notation in the book 'Argentine Tango – Class Companion'. Comments in square brackets added.

Review of this book: 'Rasche Notation':
"Thomas has produced a true shorthand that is very neat, clean and powerful for noting Argentine Tango steps. For anyone who's ever forgotten a move they loved in class, here is the answer!"
Richard Atkinson, February 2009, UK.

Reviews of the book 'Argentine Tango – Class Companion':
"...This book contains correct, precise and synthesised information... As didactic reading it can help a great deal with understanding, including the mechanics of the dance of the tango, as well as sparking the interest of the people who read it, without any previous knowledge of the dance. ..."
Damián Esell, Buenos Aires, 2007.

"The book is wonderful congratulations...
I found that your book is more than an accompaniment to dance lessons, it is a love affair with tango."
Sharon Morris, 19th July 2007

"...I can happily recommend Thomas's new book on Tango - very informative and with some very nice little drawings by Thomas of buildings and landscape. There are some complex thoughts about dancing Tango that you will want to read more than once!"
Peter Burgess, 17th July 2007

"Thomas Rasche's guide to Argentine Tango gives a descriptive account of what this dance is. The dance is intricate and the Author touches upon many of its details. He looks at its subtleties, the embrace, the energetics of its movement, the mechanics of the dance and the male and female role. I love the description of this dance as being a communication, a language...
...Thomas also shares his knowledge of musicality, dance styles, step combinations... An informative accompaniment to one's Tango journey."
Vicki, 01st March 2008. Full review appears in the e-zine Smooth Moves.

**This book is dedicated to my mother Elisabeth,
for always being there for me.**

### Acknowledgements

This book, as any other, is a result of the valuable direct and indirect contributions from many people.

I would like to thank all the members of my family, for their encouragement and support. Karen Dyer, for your time, patience and encouragement during the months this project has taken. Michele Tedder and Vicky Reynolds for the feedback, as well as putting up with my use of space. Elsa Godinho for the encouragement, many dances in Milongas and for teaching with me. Alex and Helen Morris for your feedback. David and Elisabeth Hart, and Lysanne and Jonathan Elvers. Giulia Dence for the feedback, and organising and teaching with me in Stroud. Tommi Grover of Multilingual Matters ltd. for the recommended contacts. Richard Atkinson for the review of the book.

Joaquín Amenábar for the review of the notation, both in the first publication and in its current form. Your comments and insights were very encouraging and helpful.

My thanks to Tango community as a whole, for the wonderful times dancing, and the friendships I have made. You make Tango a truly special dance.

My thanks also to you for reading this book.
I hope that it will be of great benefit to you.

### Credits
Covers by Thomas Rasche

The basis for the front cover image was a photograph by Loukia Lili, taken at an *assado* (grill evening) in Bath, UK in May 2008. Dancing in the rain are Thomas Rasche and Catherine Garrett.

Sketch on back cover and page 1, Buenos Aires Congresso (Town Hall), 2002 by Thomas Rasche

My apologies if there are any omissions or errors in this book.

# Contents

**Foreword**

Have you ever tried to remember Tango steps?
Have you ever tried to write down a Tango choreography?

After my first classes as a student, I would leave class wanting to write down and remember a step sequence. I became frustrated at the difficulty of doing this. By the time I had left a class, a few days would pass, and then going to a *Milonga* (a Tango dance evening), it would take both my partner and me quite a few minutes to remember and piece together the step again, as we had learnt it. There were her steps, there were my steps, and then also how these fitted together, and then with the music. How much better it would be, I was thinking, if there was a simple way of writing all the steps that I was learning...

At the time, I created my first notation system; it wasn't very useful, although it did work. The notation was very complex, with everything that I was learning included in it. This was fine, until I was beginning to learn more intricate steps, which then made the whole system impossible. This began a process of development, and with time, Rasche Notation emerged, and was first published in the book 'Argentine Tango – Class Companion'. This has now developed further to become this book, which you have before you.

There are other types of dance notation, including Laban and Benesh systems, which are well known (whole body) notation systems. These are often considered too general when trying to describe the intricate movements of Tango. Also, there are a few other notation types, which were specifically designed for Argentine Tango. These include Bodirsky, Castro, Dinzel and Tangotation, as well as many other discussed methods online, all of which are useful alternatives to the whole body notation methods.

The development of Rasche Notation (pronounced 'Rá-sher') builds upon the requirement for a system of notation for Argentine Tango that is easy to learn, write and read. To enable this, Rasche Notation features:

- A notation specifically designed for Argentine Tango.
- A simple writing method, using symbols readily available on computers.
- A method of reducing the quantity of writing, using generalisations.
- A method of describing the context: music and general notes.

As mentioned above, the first time Rasche Notation for Argentine Tango was published, was in the book 'Argentine Tango - Class Companion' in 2007 (see the reference chapter 'Further Information' for more details). This book was written to compliment the teaching of Tango as an introduction to its history, culture, context and more. Within this book, the chapter on notation was included as a tool to help describe some steps. However, the notation generated considerable interest, especially after extracts were put on the internet, under the name of Rasche Notation. Recognising the interest, this new book develops and expands beyond the original descriptions, with more and better explanations and examples. See the chapter 'Rasche Notation developments' for information as to how the notation has developed and changed since the first publication.

The following text abbreviates Rasche Notation to **RaNote**. Also, the word Tango is used to describe Argentine Tango (Tango Argentino), not ballroom or other styles of tango. Also, the words 'man' and 'leader' are used interchangeably, as are the words 'woman' and 'follower'. Words in italics within the text are commonly used Spanish words in Tango. The English in this book is English-English, not US-English.

Further information about Rasche Notation can also be found on the website www.RascheNotation.com. If you would like to share your thoughts and comments about Rasche Notation, you can link to a discussion forum from the website www.RascheNotation.com. Thomas can be contacted at: thomas@RascheNotation.com.

"Dance is the only art of which we ourselves
are the stuff of which it is made."
Ted Shawn 1891-1972

"When the music changes, so does the dance"
African proverb

# The basics

# 1 The philosophy of RaNote

It is useful to describe the advantages and thinking behind RaNote by asking and answering a few questions:

## 1) Can I use RaNote to remember dance steps?

RaNote is intended as an easy way help remember one's own dance steps, explaining steps to someone else and for documenting steps for others, as a choreographic tool. It does this by being a form of writing, describing the destination of each movement: as geometric snap shots in time.

## 2) Are symbols, as used in RaNote, the best way to notate dance?

The use of symbols is appropriate and useful because they are familiar, easily written and reproduced. They can succinctly represent and accurately describe geometries, concepts and complex situations.

Dance is a four-dimensional art form: three physical dimensions plus the change in time. Furthermore, Tango has two dancers interacting closely together, adding to the difficulty of notation. Any representation of dance will be selective, and will only represent part of the dance. The selective part that RaNote uses, takes from the natural advantages that Tango offers:

The movements mostly happen at one level, within the horizontal plane, whereby the feet always step onto the ground and the upper bodies remain at the same level. Therefore the movements are described in two dimensions: as if viewed from above, looking down onto a flat horizontal plane.

The movements are mostly in the legs, with the shape of the couple's embrace remaining mostly the same. Therefore, most of the symbols describe the most expressed movement: that of the feet (i.e. lower part of the body).

Dance contains fluid, circular movements, but the best method to notate and represent this is with regular snap-shots of movements. RaNote does this by describing the destination of each step or movement, but which also relate to the music counts. Brief moments of inaction are visible when the feet are placed on the ground, remaining where they are until lifted towards their next destination. These are captured with RaNote symbols. The paradox is that the feet reach out from the fluidity of the dance as the most animated part of the movement, yet they are also the parts that become grounded, albeit briefly.

Time is marked with the representation of music. By vertically aligning the music counts with the symbols on the dance lines, each movement occurs at a particular moment in time.

RaNote combines music phrases with dance phrases. The audible musical rhythms are described, as are the details of each step for each dancer.

## 3) Is RaNote simple and intuitive to write?

A dance notation for dance steps must be simple and intuitive to use: easy to learn, read and write. Simple doesn't mean simplistic, it means direct, without fussiness and without the distraction of too much detail.

RaNote does this. It uses familiar text symbols, which are either abbreviations of words or pictographic in describing an object or movement. Furthermore, it does not require complex tools or software to write them. It is written across the page, and uses standard typeset letters and symbols found when using standard computer (word processing) software. Steps can also easily be written with pen and paper, or even on a phone as a text message!

## 4) Is RaNote simple and intuitive to read?

If the notation is simple and intuitive to read, it becomes possible to dance the steps as they are read, without the need for them to be deconstructed.

RaNote does this by using familiar text symbols, together with a syntax, grammar and punctuation that is common in ordinary language. It is simply a short-hand (or condensed), version of what is already familiar. Furthermore, using RaNote economises the amount of writing so that the script and page are not cluttered, enabling fluid reading. RaNote uses assumptions to avoid repetitions of minor information, giving priority to the essentials.

## 5) Do steps written in RaNote fit to music?

It is a key part of RaNote to have both music and the steps written together.

RaNote does this with a line dedicated to the music, describing it in a simple way, to which the steps can then be referred. The steps are succinctly described so that a musical phrase can fit across a page, with both the essential musical information and all the matching step information.

## 6) Are qualities of movement, musicality and attitudes described?

Dancing Tango is more than just about the geometry; there is also a need to describe other aspects such as musicality, attitude and more.

RaNote does this with two context lines and two dance lines, which are all read together. Also, one of the context lines (Description) can include notes about musicality aspects, feelings, attitudes, qualities of movements and other context issues which cannot be described elsewhere.

## 7) Is RaNote compatible with other forms of communication?

The notation must fit comfortably with other forms of communication, and media, as well as other methods of expression such as sheet music.

RaNote does this, as it is written from left to right, with standard typeset symbols. Also, since the notation can be written using standard software, it is easy to write, display, print, copy, and edit further, either in hard copy or electronically.

## 2 What does RaNote look like?

RaNote is written from left to right, as in writing and music notation. It is split into four rows making a stave (US: staff) with a horizontal dividing line. Two rows of writing are above the dividing line and two rows of writing are below. The two rows of writing above the division are for the context (music, phrases and notes), i.e. they are context lines. The two rows of writing below the dividing line are for the detailed notation of steps, i.e. they are dance lines. The four lines are labelled as follows:

C          Compás (or Count) line, indicating the music.
D          Description line, for comments and summaries      — Dividing line
M          Man's dance line, for his steps and movements
W          Woman's dance line, for her steps and movements

The labels of the rows are C and D above the line and M and W below the line. RaNote is read across the page and simultaneous elements are vertically aligned. In other words, the step associated with a particular musical count will be written directly below it.

The rows have the following names and functions:

Above the dividing line:
**C**- the **C**ompás line, counts and/or summarises the music. The audible (and danceable) beats are counted, organised around each phrase of the music.
**D**-The **D**escription line, includes dance phrases, as well as elements that apply for all the lines. It also includes any comments, specific prompts, cues or aspects that the other lines do not cover.

Below the dividing line:
**M** and **W**- are the dance lines where the geometry of steps and movements are written, for the **M**an and the **W**oman. They are sequential snapshots in the movement destinations, and read in conjunction with the two rows above the dividing line.

It is easy to remember the above order of lines:
"Music first, played on CDs, for the man and woman!"

RaNote uses the same format of writing horizontally, from left to right, as with sentences. Also, RaNote is sequential, so that the first movements are written first, then followed by the later movements.

The recommended font for RaNote, and used in the examples in this book is Arial (size 10pt).

# 3 Understanding RaNote – it's easy!

Let us use an example of a few steps, with a progression of thoughts, to help us understand and use RaNote. It will also introduce the RaNote principles. First, let's write a step in long hand, which is the easiest way to write down a step. It would become something like:

**The man's left foot steps to the front.**
**The woman's right foot steps to the back.**

## Movement is described as (a set of) destinations

Do you notice that it is natural to describe the movements in terms of their destinations? RaNote is also used like this: destinations are always described.

## Symbols abbreviate words

Descriptions of movement, including the above sentences, are made up of words. Many of the words repeat themselves, so we can reduce some of the essential ones to symbols. This has many advantages, making the writing short, clear and quick to read and write. This is like creating a short-hand version of the sentence. Here are some of the most common symbols in RaNote (these are described in more detail in later chapters):

**M**, **W**      **M**an(-'s), **W**oman(-'s).
**L**, **R**,      **L**eft… (foot), **R**ight… (foot).
**#**      Close. The free foot steps to be next to the standing foot.
**1**…**12**      Directions are 1 to 12 as on a **clock** face, drawn around the dancers. Direction 12 is from the man's axis to the woman's axis.

## First principle: Reduce the amount of writing (there are three ways)

A key principle in RaNote is to reduce the amount of writing to the essentials. The above sentences can be (first) reduced by replacing the key words with symbols. Then (second), these are further reduced by removing non-essential words. The sentences now become 'step symbols' (a combination of more than one symbol, describing a step or movement):

First, the above sentences are reduced with symbols to:
The **M L** steps to the **12**.    … Second, these reduce to:    ML12
The **W R** steps to the **12**.    (these are 'step symbols')    WR12

Note: in later chapters, we will see that the clock directions can also be written from the woman's perspective. In short, we use brackets, so that the symbol WR12 is the same as writing WR(6). But more of this later...

Then (third), the step symbols are reduced by using assumptions. With these, step symbols are condensed: fewer symbols represent the same information. See below, as well as chapter 4 'RaNote assumptions and generalisations'.

Second principle: syntax-one rule

Looking again at the writing of steps in long hand, there is a particular order (i.e. syntax) that the words appear within the sentences. RaNote uses this same syntax for all step symbols and is the one rule to remember.

The rule describing the syntax of RaNote step symbols is:

**'What goes where'**                    (followed by extra information if needed)

So, for example, when we write MR3 this describes the Man's right foot moving to the right. Whereby MR is the 'what' (man's right foot), and 3 describes the 'goes where' (it moves to position 3, which is to the right, as he sees it, if a clock face were drawn on the ground around him).

Using these step symbols, here is an example of a few simple steps. These three steps are often called the *resolution*. We'll do this for the man first, as he leads:

ML12       MR3       ML#

The man's left foot steps forwards, then his right foot steps right and finally his left foot closes against the other foot.

We will add some woman's steps to mirror these, writing her equivalent steps underneath. If the steps are written above each other, they happen at the same time:

ML12       MR3       ML#
WR12       WL3       WR#

Reducing this information, we can keep the men's and women's steps in separate rows. This means we need not write M or W in every step symbol:

M       L12       R3       L#
W       R12       L3       R#

Now, for clarity, here are some written descriptions of the man's steps, to help explain what is happening:

| Description | Man's left forwards | Man's right steps right | Man's left closes |
|---|---|---|---|
| M | L12 | R3 | L# |
| W | R12 | L3 | R# |

Note that clock directions are relative to him (unless in brackets). Examples with clock directions in brackets on the W woman's dance line are discussed later in this book.

## Third principle: using assumptions, only unusual elements are notated

As previously mentioned, assumptions and generalisations are used in RaNote so that excessive information can be avoided, reducing the content of the RaNote lines. A principle way to do this is to have as many regular situations as possible bound into generalisations; thereby we only need to notate the unusual elements. One of these generalisations regards the clock directions written on the man's dance line: the M line. The assumption is: if no clock direction is written, it describes direction 12 (forwards). Only if this is not the case, it should be written. Therefore:

| Description | Man's left forwards | Man's right steps right | Man's left closes |
|---|---|---|---|
| M | L | R3 | L# |
| W | R12 | L3 | R# |

A further assumption applies to the clock directions written on the woman's dance line: the W line. Here, the assumption is: if no clock direction is written, the step is taken in the same direction as the man's direction (as written on the man's M dance line). This assumption is useful, as the woman generally follows the man, and takes a step in the same direction as him, mirroring his action (*espejo*). It is the direction that his upper body, or axis, moves and leads. The above line now becomes:

| Description | Man's left forwards | Man's right steps right | Man's left closes |
|---|---|---|---|
| M | L | R3 | L# |
| W | R | L | R# |

Clock directions can of course still be written, if this helps with the understanding of the steps. However, we are looking to reduce the symbols.

## Fourth principle: remove the obvious

Now let us consider that if something is obvious, then it should also be removed, to avoid clutter. An important thing to realise is that each step is described as a full step: the foot is placed <u>and</u> the weight is transferred onto it. Therefore, in the above example, to close the feet, only the trailing foot without weight can do the movement. We can assume that the feet alternate, one after the other. When one foot (e.g. L) is notated, then the following step symbol refers to the other foot (i.e. R). We can reduce the script of the above example further, while still keeping it complete:

| Description | Man's left forwards | Man's right step right | Man's left closes |
|---|---|---|---|
| M | L | R3 | # |
| W | R | L | # |

We'll leave the man's second step to be R3 for clarity. If a step symbol is reduced to just a clock direction ( 3 in this example) it looks isolated, so therefore, as a rule, all clock directions must have a preceding symbol. As a note, there is the possibility to write RS instead of R3, which can be reduced to just S. This describes a side step (part of a *giro*), but relative to his partner and not as a clock direction. The giro symbols are described in later chapters.

### Fifth principle: include the context of music

The above example is now nearly complete. What is missing is how the steps are timed, in other words how they fit to music. Let's add a time line, which we'll call the Compás line, into which we can add the timing or musical counts, called Compás counts. For more information about the Compás line, please see chapter 5 'The Compás Line – music phrases'. The timing of all steps and music can now be compared by reading their vertical alignments.

| Compás | 1 | 2 | 3 |
|---|---|---|---|
| Description | Man's left forwards | Man's step right | Man's left closes |
| M | L | R3 | # |
| W | R | L | # |

The writing can now be removed from the Description line, as this doubles the information that we have on the M line. Let's reserve the Description line for other comments, such as context, notes and dance phrases. Since this step is called *resolution*, we'll write this in the Description line. The Compás and Description can be reduced to C and D. Finally, the RaNote line is complete:

| C | 1 | 2 | 3 |
|---|---|---|---|
| D | Resolution | | |
| M | L | R3 | # |
| W | R | L | # |

This reduces into a smaller space, to be complete, neat and easy to read:

| C | 1 | 2 | 3 |
|---|---|---|---|
| D | Resolution | | |
| M | L | R3 | # |
| W | R | L | # |

Here are two other helpful ways to consider the four lines of the stave:
-The Compás line describes the audible (music), the Description line describes kinaesthetic (the intention and practical aspect of the movement). The dance lines describe the (visual) detail, of each movement's destination.
-The Context lines show locations and destinations, the dance lines describe how to get between them. The difference is the time attributed between the symbols. The Description lines show phrases and the dance lines show steps.

## More RaNote symbols

Tango steps can become more interesting as the two dancers move together and around each other. There are some very useful methods and symbols available in RaNote that help to describe this. These include the summary of the dance phrases, as well as numerous other symbols that represent the *giro* (turn) steps, the interaction between the couple and more.

The *giro* steps are used to describe steps relative to the partner, rather than the clock directions (which is refers to the inter-axis line). The *giro* symbols describe steps when going around the partner, with the assumption that the distance within the couple remains the same. The symbols for these steps are:

S              an inside side step, across the partner.
F              a forwards step, across the partner.
$              an outside side step across the partner (with a pivot).
B              a back step across the partner (with a pivot).

The *giro* steps are commonly taught in Tango, as they are a natural progression when stepping around a partner. The symbols S and F are the steps where the free foot moves between the dancers (inside) and the symbols $ and B are where the free foot moves behind the standing leg (i.e. around the outside). See also chapter 12 'Diagrams: Giro steps'.

Other useful symbols in RaNote describe the phases within a step. A full step is assumed to include a foot placement and the movement onto it. If this is not done, it is not a step. Instead, symbols can describe part of a step: to describe the foot collects c (it only moves towards the axis, no weight transfers onto it), the foot projects p (no weight transfers), or once placed there is partial ∩, or full ∏ subsequent weight transfer onto it.

There are also symbols that qualify the Tango steps, including a change in length of a step, their timing and slurs to describe fluidity.

Also, there are symbols that substitute wordy descriptions and circumstances for further information, including a step between the partner's feet %, the embrace ¥, contact with =, legs Ω and more.

Furthermore, there is a simple grammar and method to make the symbols easier and clearer to read. These include punctuation, superscript, subscript, bold text, italics and bracketed information.

To see all the symbols, together with fuller explanations about all of them, see chapter 7 'The Man and Woman dance lines – step symbols', as well as the chapters with examples and diagrams.

## 4 RaNote assumptions and generalisations

By assuming some situations to always apply to the notation, we can significantly reduce the amount of information we need to write down. The principle is to capture as much information into assumptions and generalisations, and then only the exceptions need to be notated or described. The following are the generalisations and assumptions used in RaNote:

1) The main assumption is that the reader has knowledge of Tango. This enables the writer of RaNote to only write the essentials of steps, rather than every detail, including all the subtleties, as that would be impossible. This greatly economises the volume of writing needed to describe the dance.

2) The assumption is that the man leads, and the woman follows. Therefore, the M line is for the man, but can be understood as the leader line, and the W line is for the woman, but can be understood as the follower's line. The man leads so that the woman is able to do her steps as noted (and vice versa). In other words, when dancing the notated steps, she's following his lead rather than following the choreography. The symbol € (lead to enable the partner to...) need therefore not be used often: it only explicitly describes the lead.

3) All clock directions are as seen by the man, relative to the inter-axis line, as he indicates and leads the direction of the dance. This is the case if written on the M or W line. If, however, the clock directions are in brackets on the W line, these clock directions are as seen from her perspective.

4) On the Man's M line, if no clock direction is written, the assumption is that the clock direction is 12 (straight ahead). For example, L is a forwards step with the left, the same as writing L12.
Note, some variations to this apply for the symbols #, c and T.

5) On the Woman's W line, if no clock direction is written, the assumption is that the direction is the same as the man, as written on the M line. In other words, she mirrors (*espejo*) the same direction that he (his axis) takes.

6) Steps are taken with alternate feet. When one foot (e.g. L) is notated, then the next notation refers to the other foot (e.g. R). This may seem obvious, but with this becoming an assumption, the need for writing repeated L, R, L in step symbols is reduced (to what becomes understandable).

7) Movement is continuous and smooth from one step to the next. Each step that is described is complete, including the *collect*, balance, projection, placement <u>and</u> weight transfer phases. The step therefore ends with the weight over the foot which has been described.

8) The step symbols are a reasonable approximation of the geometries of steps; a perfect representation is never possible. If the reader has knowledge of Tango, and the movements (feet) are described, this is sufficient to read and then reproduce the dance. The step symbols describe the destination(s) of the movement(s), as seen from the previous position.

9) The step symbols are reduced to a minimum wherever possible, thereby saving space and enabling easier reading. Only essential movements are described with a step symbol and not every detail. With this enabling the main movement, some accommodating secondary movements could also take place, but these need not be written - they can be assumed. The writer, however, may include more symbols, if it makes the notated steps easier to understand.

10) The shape of the embrace is assumed to remain constant. The communication, through the Tango embrace, remains the same, even if there are subtle changes to accommodate the geometries of the steps (e.g. opening, closing and rotation of the embrace). The symbol ¥ can describe the embrace in more detail.

11) Symbols describing the destination positions of the feet will thereby imply the positions of the legs. Otherwise, the symbol Ω describes the legs.

12) The timing of steps is indicated with the vertical alignment of dance step symbols beneath the Compás line symbols. To be exact, the starts of these symbols are aligned. The step symbols describe the destinations for each step; therefore the timing assumes that the <u>placement</u> of the feet on the ground coincide with the symbols on the Compás line. Variations of this are explained in chapter 19 'Musicality'.

13) If there is a space before a step symbol, this acts to indicate a new movement. In this case, a full stop is not required.

14) The starting position is not normally described, and is assumed to be such that the first step(s) becomes possible. It will typically be a standing position with the feet together and the weight on one side, usually with the man standing on his right side (the woman on her left).

15) The axis of any rotation is vertical (even if the person is sloped).

16) The writer of a choreography using RaNote has the freedom to use, include and exclude symbols, as well as to create and define symbols as makes sense for his readers. It is an open system of notation.

"What saves a man is to take a step. Then another step.
It is always the same step, but you have to take it."
Antoine de Saint-Exupéry 1900-1944


"...he hears a different drummer. Let him step to the music
which he hears, however measured or far away."
Henry David Thoreau 1817-1862

# The lines within RaNote

## 5 The Compás Line – music phrases

The word Compás in Spanish means rhythm or meter, the cyclic rhythms of the music. In RaNote, the Compás line is used to notate and describe the music, and is the top line of the RaNote stave. The Compás symbols are all the numbers, letters, symbols and words written on the Compás line.

To write a dance requires not only the steps, but also the music to which the steps refer, thereby describing changes in time. To be able to write down the music, we could simply say that the steps are to be written together with sheet music. Although this is possible, it is not practical, as sheet music is not always available and is difficult (or slow) to read unless you have some musical training. Therefore, what is required is a method to condense the music that you hear into a shorter and more accessible form. To do this, it is useful to understand how a piece of music is constructed. This then enables us to take the essential elements from it, and use it in RaNote notation.

Overall, a piece of music has layers of structure within it, which reduce in scale. A piece of music is recognizable for its succession of notes (i.e. its melody). A melody is built up with a succession of phrases, which are comparable to written or spoken sentences. They are the expression of a thought or statement; a phrase has a comparable length and it is clear when it ends. In music, a cadence is audible punctuation, making the ending of a phrase very clear.

The structure of a piece of music will combine these phrases in a particular way, and this creates the music form. The form is the overall construction of the musical piece, with musical phrases grouped into a few sections.

Making an analogy with the written (or spoken) word, a musical phrase is comparable to a sentence. The form of the music can be compared to how chapters and paragraphs organize text. Furthermore, bars and notes can be compared to words and individual letters within a sentence. The punctuation (comma/ full stop) within a sentence compare to cadences, of which there are different types in writing and music. This analogy is helpful for understanding, but becomes laboured if followed too far (for example, music can be more layered and simultaneous than language).

Detailed discussions of various structural elements within music theory are beyond the scope of this book. Instead, we use a practical method for describing the music. See chapter 'Further information' for music theory.

The RaNote method of writing the music on the Compás line makes use of some of the elements of music structure, which are most easily heard and understood when listening to a piece of music. These are parts that a musically un-trained person can also distinguish, making it very useful for all

dancers and choreographers. The elements within music that are used in the RaNote method are:
1) Form (for the orientation within a piece of music).
2) Phrase (for useful subdivisions of the music: the sentences in music).
3) Audible count within each phrase (to locate the timing of each step).

Note that there are parts of the music which are not essential to RaNote and only exceptionally noted. These include: Pitch, Melody and melodic components (including Motifs), Themes, Phrase Structure, Key, Key signatures, Instruments, Volume, Singing and Lyrics.
Cadences are indirectly noted, whereby every phrase will naturally end with a cadence. The types of musical cadences are not described. Rhythm is reduced to the essential count throughout the music.

Let's look at the above mentioned elements in more detail, to see how they appear in RaNote:

1) Form
The purpose of understanding and noting the form of the music assists in finding our location within the piece of music.

A piece of music is constructed in various sections, making the form. Each section has a particular character, some of which repeat. Recognising these makes the understanding and labelling of the music much easier.

Each section, within the form, is labelled using letters: A, B, C... .
Any repeated sections will use the same letter again.

Typical forms in Tango music include ABACA (the form of a sonata and rondo), often heard in the *guarda vieja*, or ABA, often heard in a *canción*. A sonata form consists of the exposition, development and recapitulation.

The repeated letters identify the repeated sections within the music. To distinguish whether it is the first time the section is played, or is a repeat, a subscript number helps in its identification and therefore with orientation within the piece of music. The first time section A is played, it need only be labelled as A. The subsequent repeat of A is then labelled $A_2$ (the second time it's played). This then is followed by $A_3$ etc.

A label or tag is put onto each Compás line, which then identifies the row within the form of the music. However, since each section within the form is quite long, containing a few phrases, each label will also need to include a reference to each phrase. This way, phrases can then be uniquely identified.

## 2) Phrase

A phrase, as mentioned, is equivalent in length to a sentence of speech. The lengths of phrases are repeated throughout a piece of music. For clarity, the intention is to fit one phrase onto one row of notation, thereby, if we uniquely identify each musical phrase, we also identify each row of notation.

To label the phrases within the music, the easiest way might be to simply number the phrases through from 1 until, say, 20. However, just counting the phrases through does not take advantage of the music's form, which also helps in orientation within the music.

Therefore, combining the letters labelling the form, together with the numbering of the phrases, we get:

A1, A2, A3, A4,  B1, B2, B3, B4...

Whereby it is clear that here the first section (label prefix A) has four phrases (numbered 1 to 4), which is followed by the second section (label prefix B), which also has four phrases (numbered 1 to 4).

If a section were to repeat, the letters of the form receive a sequence number in subscript:

A1, A2, A3, A4,  B1, B2, B3, B4,  $A_2$1, $A_2$2, $A_2$3, $A_2$4

Where $A_2$3 would describe 'the second section A, third phrase'.
If there is no number, we can assume that the phrase is the first of its type.

Each of these labels would then be written at the start of each Compás line, identifying each musical phrase, and, since there's one phrase per row, each row is also identified. These labels refer to the music, which is why they are written on the Compás line, rather than on the Description, or other, line.

We now have a typical RaNote stave with a label. They are called phrase labels. The phrase label is written in bold text for prominence, at the start of the musical phrase:

C  **A3**
D _____
M
W

### 3) Compás count: the simple, regular, audible rhythm of each phrase.

A phrase is the most important construction within the music for the purposes of RaNote and to write a choreography, as well as extremely useful to understand the music that one listens and dances to. The reason is that a phrase has the right amount of time to which one you can fit a step sequence. Therefore, once a phrase is recognised, it needs to be described sufficiently, so that the steps of a step sequence can fit to it. To do this, it is not necessary to understand the underlying theory of music. What is required for the Compás line is the Compás count, which is the <u>regular</u> count, audible and accented beats of a phrase.

The Compás count typically consists of eight counts per phrase. In ballroom dancing, these are the 'slow' counts. Music theory would describe this as simple time, which is where the beats of a bar (US: Measure) are divided in twos. So, taking a bar written in 4/4 time (4 beats), it is the first and third beats that are accented: **1** 2 **3** 4. Phrases are often four bars long, each with two accented beats; hence the typical phrase has a Compás count of **8**. Less common is Tango music using compound time (divided into three), or with different time signatures. For further explanations of the differences between simple and compound time, please refer to music theory resources. Important to realise is if music is played at a normal tempo, simple time has the speed of steps when walking. The Compás count has a comfortable, regular tempo.

We count the regular, audible, accented beats of a phrase, i.e. the Compás count, and these are the beats to which the dancers can comfortably step to the music. The Compás count will usually look as follows, when written on the Compás line (the accented musical beats are in the Description line):

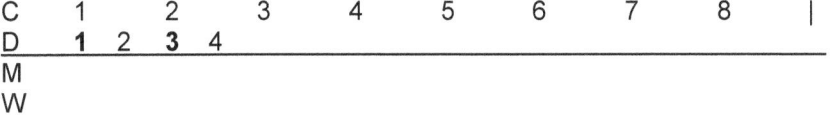

This Compás count of 8 is important for RaNote, and with it, the underlying theory of the music need not be known. The Compás count is the most important construct in the Compás line, and is the point of reference for all the other rhythms (and steps).

When writing RaNote, the underlying Compás count will usually be the same throughout the piece. This knowledge makes it easy to then copy the Compás count (1 to 8 as in the above example) into each phrase, and thereby creating the framework of the piece of music.

The '|' line is used to clearly mark the end of a phrase. However, the assumption is that a new phrase will begin on a new line, so the symbol will only need to be used at the end of a phrase, if it is not a line break.

## 4) Alternative accented rhythms: double or half time.

A piece of music can have a variety of rhythms, as is often the case with Tango music. The regular, audible rhythm or counts will differ from the Compás count (simple time). This includes faster and slower rhythms, which are played at double (or half of) the speed of simple time. These are appropriately called double or half time. To mark these rhythms in the Compás line, the Compás count is adjusted to reflect the audible rhythm.

If the accented beats are half as frequent compared to the Compás count (simple time), then it is called half time. Taking a bar in 4/4 time (4 beats), it is only the first beat that is accented: **1** 2 3 4. The Compás count on the Compás line is then changed to become:

      1    -    3    -    5    -    7    -

The hyphens suggest a beat can be counted, but is not audibly accented. The underlying structure of 8 Compás counts remains the same for all the phrases of the whole piece of music.

If the all the beats of a bar are audible, the accented beats are at double the tempo of the Compás count in simple time, therefore this is called double time. When this is the case, the extra beats between the Compás counts are audible. These extra in-between beats are added to the Compás line. In ballroom dancing, these are the 'quick' counts. Taking a bar in 4/4 time (4 beats), all are accented: **1 2 3 4**. The Compás count on the Compás line is then changed to become:

    1 and 2 and 3 and 4 and 5 and 6 and 7 and 8 and

The word **and** can be reduced to the symbol **&** to save space.

A Compás line may now, depending on the music it describes, appear as:

    1 & 2 & 3 & 4 & 5    -    7    -

A piece of music can now be described using the Compás count in simple time, and then edited to reflect whether the rhythm is played in half or double time. Important is that the underlying structure of the Compás count remains visible, as this is important for the orientation within the piece of music.

## 5) Off-beats, syncopation and contra-time

Similar to what is described above, variations on the accented rhythms or any extra beats can also be marked into the Compás line. Again, this is done by editing the Compás count according to what is audible in the music.

If the off-beats are accented, say, in the second part of a phrase, it can be written with and or &. The Compás counts are then not accented:

$$1 \qquad 2 \qquad 3 \qquad 4 \qquad 5 \; \& \; - \; \& \; - \; \& \; - \; \&$$

If the music has extra in-between beats or rhythms, i.e. syncopations, these can also be added in:

$$1 \; a \; \& \; a \; 2 \; a \; \& \; a \; 3... \qquad \text{the same as} \qquad 1 \; ' \; \& \; ' \; 2 \; ' \; \& \; ' \; 3...$$

If the audible rhythm is not regular, the Compás line can also be adjusted accordingly so that it matches what is heard. The key is the underlying Compás count. For example, a RaNote row may now look as follows, including stave, music phrase label and Compás count:

```
C A3  1      -      3      -      5      6      7    &'8   &
D  _____
M
W
```

Or, if it is a more complex syncopated rhythm (e.g. 3-3-2), it could also be described around the Compás count:

```
C A3  1 ²³¹  2 ³¹² 3      4      5    ' 6    ' 7      8
D  _____
M
W
```

Visible is the regular underlying Compás count of the phrase as well as the two irregular rhythms. In practical terms, the danceable count is usually only simple, double or half time. The aim is to recognise the syncopations.

The word **and** can be reduced to the symbol **&** to save space.
The letter **a** can also be reduced to the symbol **'** to save space.

As a note, some Tango music may add in (an) extra musical bar(s) at the start or end of sections within the form. If this is the case, it is a matter of adding extra number onto the Compás count at the relevant phrase. Once written into the notation, it is then clear to read the exceptional phrase lengths. This depends on the structural rules and type of music that is being played. See also the reference chapter 'Further information', for music theory.

## 6) Styles of music

When initially creating Compás lines to a piece of music, it is a matter of first deciding on the Compás count. Then, once decided and copied into every line, listen to the music and highlight, cross out or add the accented beats that vary from this regular Compás count. The music phrases then become understandable and, together with phrase labels, easy to follow throughout.

There are audibly different rhythms between Tango, *Vals* (Waltz) and *Milonga* music. The Compás count can still be used equally effectively for these. A *Vals* can have the same form and phrase structure as a Tango, only the in-between beats of the Compás count differ. A *Vals* Compás line can be written as follows (the *Vals* rhythm is included in the Description line):

```
C 1 ² ³ 2 ² ³ 3 ² ³ 4 ² ³ 5 ² ³ 6 ² ³ 7 ² ³ 8 ² ³
D 1 2 3 1 2 3
M
W
```

A *Milonga* can also have a similar form and phrase structure to Tango; it also has a regular Compás count. It is the structure of the beats that define a *Milonga*, which are the in-between beats of the Compás count. *Milonga*s have an asymmetric $1$ - $_{and}3$ $4$ rhythmical sound of each musical bar (beats corresponding to the Compás count in bold). A *traspié* (trip or stumble) is stepping to the count, as well as on an asymmetric in-between beat (either on count '4' or on '$_{and}$'). A *Milonga* Compás line might appear as follows (the rhythmical sound and two examples of *traspié* steps are included on the Description line):

```
C    1     ' 2  &  3     ' 4  &  5     ' 6  &  7    ' 8  &
D    1   and3  4           <traspié>     <trp. >
M                          L  #  L       R.#  R
W
```

*Vals*es and *Milonga*s are often played faster, at a higher tempo, so that the detailed rhythm is difficult to dance to. If this is the case, again, only the simple Compás count of the phrase is needed (and is useful):

```
C    1     2     3     4     5     6     7     8
D
M
W
```

Once the Compás counts have been edited to the audible beats, the dance steps are then written directly below them. To be exact, the start of a step symbol describing a step is vertically aligned below the Compás line symbol.

## 7) Complex rhythm styles

Some modern Tango music makes use of complex rhythms throughout the piece, rather than in one section (as described in section 5 above). In this case, the structure of the music will still divide into its form and phrases. The difficulty arises in describing the rhythms simply. If, for example a 3-3-2 rhythm is used as the underlying rhythm, then the Compás count could appear very complex and be difficult to read. So, we can review how we write the Compás count: its purpose to count the regular audible rhythm (regular, but asymmetric). For extra clarity, the first count of an irregular cyclic rhythm can be written in bold text:

```
C   1     2     3  4      5    6  7     8    9  10    11    12...
D    1 2 3 1  2 3 1 2  1 2 3 1...
M
W
```

Here, the 3-3-2 rhythm is described on the Description line. The Compás counts align with the audible 1 counts of the 3-3-2 rhythm. This rhythm has a slow-slow-quick-slow-slow-quick sound. Note that the underlying structure is regular: $3+3+2 = 8$ counts. The regular rhythm is only accented asymmetrically ( **1** 2 3 4 **5** 6 7 8 becomes **1** 2 3 4 **5** 6 7 8 ).

An example of an irregular accented rhythm is Astor Piazzolla's Libertango. However, the piece overlays the irregular rhythm with phrases formed out of regular counts. Therefore, since the Compás counts reflect the phrase (what we dance to), only a regular 1 to 8 Compás count is needed. But, you do hear an underlying irregular 3-3-2 fast tempo rhythm in the music.

**Summary of symbols used on the Compás line:**

| | |
|---|---|
| **A2, A₂2** | Phrase labels, identifying each phrase within the music form. The letter indicates the section and the subscript indicates if it's a repeat. Numbers indicate the phrase within each section. |
| 1,2,3,4,5… | The regular Compás counts within a phrase. |
| \| | Indicates the end of a phrase. This is not required if the end of a phrase coincides with the end of a row. |
| - | Non-accented Compás count. |
| and, & | Half count beats (between the rhythmical counts). |
| a | Quarter count beats. |
| ' | Any other irregular (or faster) beats/counts. |
| **Bold** | Bold text, highlights a particular symbol, count or beat in the music. Phrase labels are highlighted this way. |
| Superscript | Can be used for clarity to describe extra details or notes, or in place of round brackets. |
| ½,⅓,⅞ | Fractions for indicating parts of the music (rhythm). |
| ♪ | A symbol abbreviating the Compás count. |

## 6 The Description Line – dance phrases and notes

The Description line contains notes and symbols that relate to the whole dance, i.e. it is a place for universal descriptions. Also, the dance phrase descriptions and any symbols that do not belong, or out of place, on either the Compás or dance lines of the notation, are written on the Description line.

For example, the names of steps can be written into the Description line. Also, musical terms might be included to describe a feeling, which are also interpreted into the movements of the dancers, similar to music notation. Therefore, descriptions such as: brio (I: vigour/animation), dolce (I: soft), kräftig (G: strong), legato (I: smooth), marcato (I: emphatic/accented), mesto (I: sad), scherzando (I: playful/joking), etc. belong on the Description line.

All contextual notes also belong on the Description line. These can include notes about cues to listen or watch for, the stage location, choreographic features, as well as any other elements of interest for a choreography. There is enough space on the Description line to write things long-hand. To emphasise something, such as a cue, it can be highlighted in **bold** text. Bold text is used for highlighting important parts throughout the notation.

Both the locations and orientation on stage are put on the Description line. The locations on stage are described with abbreviations for Centre **C**, Left **L**, Right **R**, Up stage **U** and **D**own stage **D**, from the performer's perspective. The orientation on stage is described with the stage symbol § together with a clock direction. For more information, see chapter 9 'Diagrams: Clock directions for stage'

A fundamental part of Tango is the shape of the embrace. It is the origin of various dance styles and it is therefore useful to describe it, in the Description line. As steps are made, the shape of the embrace will change to accommodate the movements, but the embrace will usually return to the original default shape when possible. Therefore, the embrace need only be described once, at the start. Only if the default embrace changes, is it noted.

The symbol ¥ is used to describe the embrace. Embrace information can then be added, and here are examples: ¥(open) open embrace (same for closed), or ¥(mil.) as in the milonguero style. A lean is described as ¥(/), or ¥(∧) together, ¥(V) apart, or ¥(|||) independent. Usually, an embrace has a slight angle and the feet are offset. If not, the embrace can be described as ¥(parallel) and ¥(opposite). The head positions can be described as looking over each other's shoulders ¥(● ☺), or facing the same way ¥(☺ ☺). The symbol ¥(↔) describes the embrace separates. The symbols ˥, ˦ and ☺ describe left arm, right arm and head positions. See also chapter 7 'The Man and Woman dance lines – step symbols' for the rotation of one person within the embrace, using the ¥ symbol, e.g. ¥(6).

Dance Phrase

The two context lines above the dividing line of RaNote are there to describe the general and context issues of the dance. As previously described, the Compás line does this for the music, summarising it neatly: into sections and phrases; it then represents the music according to the audible and danceable rhythm. The Description line has been left for all context and general notes.

Steps are taught and described with names, but these tend to be more as family names, rather than a specific sequence of steps. For example, a step sequence may be called *salida*, and this is written in the Description line above the step symbols. However, different dancers and teachers will do a *salida* in various ways.

There is a requirement to describe step sequences: less detailed than step symbols, but more detailed than names given to a step sequence. What needs to be described is the dance phrase, and the best place to write this is the Description line.

A dance phrase is another name for a step sequence. We can compare a dance phrase with a music phrase or a sentence of speech, and they usually have a similar length (step sequences fit to music). It ends with a cadence, or a stop.

Writing a dance phrase enables quicker understanding of the shape of the steps by grouping steps together. The dance phrase is indicated and framed with the {...} symbols, and includes what it is (name or description), when it is to be danced (start) and when it's completed (end). If a dance phrase is written into the RaNote stave (on the Description line), it can benefit from its context: it can be directly compared to the Compás line for music, which shows how long it takes, and to the dance lines for the detailed steps symbols. Within the RaNote stave, a dance phrase description will look as follows:

| C | 1 | - | 3 | - | 5 | - | 7 | - |
|---|---|---|---|---|---|---|---|---|
| D | | | {name | | | | } | |
| M | | | L | | R | | # | |
| W | | | R | | L | | # | |

By looking at the above example, we can see:
-the start of the dance phrase is indicated with the { symbol,
-the dance phrase begins on Compás count: 3 aligns with the { symbol,
-the the dance phrase ends on Compás count: 7 aligns with the } symbol,
-both the man and woman take three steps as part of the dance phrase,
-the three steps of both dancers match three audible Compás counts,
-the man starts with his left, and the woman starts with her right,
-the dance phrase has a label (where name is written), and
-the detail of the dance phrase is described in the dance lines: the man takes two forwards steps and a close, which the woman mirrors.

31

## RaNote Dance Phrase Description

In the above example, the label of the phrase is where {name is written. In this location, it is also possible to add extra information: a dance phrase description. This description is useful if a better summary of the steps is required. Here is what and how the information can be added:

The { symbol has a dual purpose:
-a symbol that indicates a dance phrase, and
-it is an opening bracket.

As its first purpose, the { symbol indicates a dance phrase and is used with the same syntax as all other symbols: 'what goes where'. Therefore, it is the 'what...' part of the syntax, and it is followed by the '...goes where' destination.

As its second purpose, it is an open bracket (indicating the start of the dance phrase). It must therefore be balanced with a close bracket } a bit later in the notation. The dance phrase can then be seen in its entirety, from start to finish. Furthermore, acting as a bracket, it negates the need for extra information to be in brackets. A name can therefore be included, without it also being enclosed in brackets, as long as the notation is clear to understand.

Question: according to the first purpose of the { phrase symbol, it describes the 'what...' part of the dance phrase, what can be described with the following '...goes where' symbols or words? This is an opportunity to summarise the destination of the step sequence or dance phrase. This destination can be described with either a clock direction (the couple move forwards/sideways and do not rotate), as a rotation (the couple rotate with a few steps), no destination (no movement), or the destination is unspecified.

To broadly describe a step, it is important to realise that the dance phrase description will be read in conjunction with details of the steps, which are written in the dance lines. Therefore, the purpose of the description is to show the (one) most important shape of the movement only. It does not have to be exact, as this detail is offered on the dance lines. Here are some examples of destinations for the dance phrase:

{-      }   The dancers do not move from their location.
{       }   The dancers walk forwards (assume clock direction 12), or, this could simply frame a phrase, with an unspecified destination. The details are seen in the dance lines.
{11     }   The dancers move to clock direction 11: forwards and left (a bit).
{C+     }   The dancers rotate clockwise, by stepping round or on the spot.

As part of the second purpose of the { symbol, it is an opening bracket, which must then be followed by a closing bracket. As brackets, they can include other information, such as words, notes or the name of the step. It is at the discretion of the writer to decide what to include. Here are some suggestions:

| | | |
|---|---|---|
| { | } | No information, the brackets just frame the dance phrase, indicating the start and end of the movement. This could also indicate a forward walk, and with one glance at the dance lines it is easy to see which interpretation is applicable. |
| {∂C- | } | Anticlockwise rotation with ∂ dynamic ('...goes...') energy. |
| {C+ giro | } | Dancers rotate clockwise, doing a *giro* step. |
| {C+ Wgiro | } | The woman does a clockwise *giro*, around/with the man. |

Furthermore, within the brackets, even more summarised information about the steps is possible. This is needed if the dance lines are complex. The further information that is of use includes the number of steps taken (complete, i.e. including weight transfer), and which is the starting foot. Here is a syntax for this specific information (only used in the context of the dance phrase descriptions). The syntax has four components, all written together:

**(M steps)      (start foot)      (W steps)      x (if crossed)**

This is the order of information: the number of (complete) steps the man takes, then his starting foot, followed by the number of (complete) steps the woman takes, and lastly whether it's crossed walking.

We make an assumption: the man's starting foot will be opposite to the woman's starting foot (in other words, the dancers are not in the crossed walking system). Only if they are crossed the x is added at the end.

Here are some examples, to make this shorthand clearer:

4L4    The man takes 4 four complete steps, starting with his L left foot.
       The woman also takes 4 four complete steps, starting with her right, since we assume she will start with the opposite foot.

3R4x   The man takes 3 three steps, starting with his R right foot.
       The woman takes 4 four steps, starting with her right foot (the x indicates this).

3R4    The man takes 3 three steps, starting with his R right foot.
       The woman takes 4 four steps, starting with her left foot.

7R7x   The man takes 7 seven steps, starting with his R right foot.
       The woman takes 7 seven steps, starting with her right foot x.

## Rasche Notation

Examples of complete dance phrase descriptions, with detailed information, are shown below. The information is too much for simple steps, but becomes useful with more complicated sequences. These examples illustrate the possibilities. It is up to the writer to decide the extent of these notes, and whether the dance phrase warrants all or only part of this information.

| C | 1 | - | 3 | - | 5 | - | 7 | - |
|---|---|---|---|---|---|---|---|---|
| D |   |   | { walk 3L3 |   |   |   | } |   |
| M |   |   | L |   | R |   | # |   |
| W |   |   | R |   | L |   | # |   |

| C | 1 | - | 3 | - | 5 | - | 7 | - |
|---|---|---|---|---|---|---|---|---|
| D | {2 resolution 3L3 |   |   |   | } |   |   |   |
| M | L |   | RS |   | # |   |   |   |
| W | R |   | L |   | # |   |   |   |

| C | 1 | - | 3 | - | 5 | - | 7 | - |
|---|---|---|---|---|---|---|---|---|
| D | {C+ sandwich 5L3 |   |   |   |   |   | }sandw. |   |
| M | LS | # | LS |   | R=(WL) |   | L#= |   |
| W | R |   | LB |   | RB∩ |   | - |   |

In the sandwich step example, it is quick to read from the Description line that the couple rotate clockwise (C+), but this only indicates the form of the step, it is not exact. Also, it is clear that the man takes five steps, starting with his left, and the woman takes three, starting with her right. This is not as easy to read from the dance lines. Actually, the woman only takes 2½ steps since her weight is not fully transferred by the end, but we've rounded this to 3. The details are clear in the dance lines. Furthermore, comparing the Description line with the Compás line, it is clear that the man takes an extra in-between-beat step, and the woman must take one less, as the phrase matches the length of four counts. The italics of the dance phrase separate it from the rest of the stave and helps readability. The word sandw. is written, just as a general note, to mark the point when the complete sandwich position is arrived at.

With the use of RaNote dance phrase descriptions, the stave now includes the intention of the dancers. The whole RaNote stave is therefore divided above and below the dividing line, whereby the information above includes: the Compás line describing the music phrases and the Description line containing the dance phrases, as well as general information. Below the dividing line, the detailed steps of the individual dancers are written on the Man and Woman dance lines. For more information about dance phrases, see also chapter 18 'How to write, transcribe and choreograph using RaNote'.

**Summary of symbols used on the Description line**:

| | |
|---|---|
| Rpt. | Repeat of..., the whole phrase (stave row) is repeated. If this is written at the start of the row, it describes the repeat of a previous phrase e.g. Rpt.$A_2$2. If it is written at the end of the row, then that row is repeated. |
| **C+, C-** | Clockwise, Anticlockwise rotation (of the couple). |
| ═══ | A doubled dividing line in the stave is an articulation mark describing the structure of the dance phrasing, used to group some steps together into one fluid movement. Comparable to a slur, as used in musical notation. See chapter 19 'Musicality'. |
| § | Stage symbol. Use with abbreviations of stage locations, incl.: Centre C, Left L, Right R, Up stage U and Down stage D. |
| Superscript | An alternative to round brackets, as it saves space. |
| { ... } | RaNote dance phrase: symbol and bracket (sometimes *italics*). |

Any description (text, symbols, words, lyrics etc.) are suited for the Description line. It's up to the choreographer to choose what to write, according to what needs to be understood. Here are some further suggestions:

| | |
|---|---|
| Mel. | Attention to melodic elements. |
| Rhy. | Attention to rhythmical elements (other than the counts). |
| Intro. | Text to describe other elements (introduction). |
| Dolce | How to interpret the steps (soft). |
| ¥(mil.) | Embrace (*Milonguero* style). |

In Tango, the same steps can be danced in different ways depending on various styles. The names of these styles can be used in the Description line to describe an emphasis on particular aspects, for example: the embrace, step sizes, musicality, circular or linear movements, being understated or flamboyant. Some different styles include:

Tango Canyengue is an early Tango style with smaller steps. Tango Orillero is an upright (out of town) style where space was available and kicks and flicks are possible, as opposite to the urban Tango del Centro. Tango Salon is a smooth, musical style, resulting from limited space in the city's dance halls. The emphasis is on musicality, embrace, walking and improvising. Its origins included the Petitero (small step) style, and developments include certain localities e.g. Villa Urquiza and Confiteria styles. Tango Apilado is a style where the balance is interdependent, with a leaning posture, also known as the Milonguero style. This is different to the independent (but connected) balance in Tango Nuevo, a modern style of Tango dancing. It has an open, elastic embrace with the emphasis on axes (balance and rotation). Show Tango has expressive moves and is choreographed (unlike Fantasia which is improvised). Tango Fusion is a combination of Tango with other dance types.

## 7 The <u>M</u>an and <u>W</u>oman dance lines – step symbols

RaNote uses two types of symbols. The first type is an abbreviation of a word (such as M for Man and W for Woman). These are an adaptation of writing the steps in long hand. The second type of symbol is pictographic (or symbolic), which is as near as a font symbol can represent what is happening. For example :-) is often used to represent a smiling face. Similarly, # represents the feet closing, or % represents a step between the partner's feet.

Symbols are used and noted in RaNote to describe the destination of each step taken by the dancers. These are written on the relevant RaNote dance lines. The step symbols are written using the syntax of 'What goes where' as described in chapter 3 'Understanding RaNote - it's easy!'. Further explanations are also in the diagrams and examples chapters.

Essential symbols:

| | |
|---|---|
| **M, W** | Man(-'s), Woman(-'s). |
| **L, R** | Left… (foot), Right… (foot). |
| **1…12** | Clock directions are written 1 to 12 as on a clock face as if drawn on the ground around the dancers. See illustration in chapter 8 'Diagrams: Clock directions'. Clock directions must be preceded by a symbol, describing what is moving. The direction of 12 is along the inter-axis line ‡ i.e. 12 is from the man's axis towards the woman's axis. This is so, even if the numbers are written on the Woman's line, unless: |
| **(1)…(12)** | Directions 1 to 12 are written in brackets, meaning relative to the person on who's line the symbol is written (i.e. on the woman's line); they are relative to her (direction 12 towards the partner's axis along the ‡ inter-axis line). For her 9 is the same as (3) or $^3$. |
| **#** | Close. The free foot steps to be next to the standing foot. See chapter 11 'Diagrams: Close steps' for use with clock directions. |
| **C+, C-** | Lower body pivots: Clockwise, Anticlockwise, (or rotation info.). |
| **%** | Step between partner's feet (or info.: inside of). |

Symbols describing the quality of the step:

| | |
|---|---|
| **-** | No movement (i.e. Freeze, the position is held). |
| **>, < … >** | Continuation of a step, or enclose a continuous movement. |
| **!, ?** | Movement is ahead, or delayed (relative to partner). |
| ___ | Underline, taken as a longer or bigger step. |
| :..... | Underline dots, taken as a smaller step (often implied in context). |

Complex Symbols (multiple movements):

These are symbols which condense information so that one symbol contains many movements, therefore, making them complex symbols.

These include the four steps of a turn (*giro*), which are complex steps of multiple movements, describing the step direction and the associated torsion and pivots. These symbols are particularly useful, as they describe a placement position relative to the partner's position, as opposed to absolute clock directions, they step across the partner. The four steps are:

**S**  Side step. A side step is sometimes called an open step.

**F**  **F**orward step. This step includes Torsion (a twist in the waist), so that the step crosses forwards, between the dancers. This forwards step is sometimes called a forwards crossed step.

**$**  Side step (with a pivot, hence **$** to distinguish it from the normal side step without torsion). The pivot is done first, with the straightening up of Torsion (so that the embrace remains). Then a side step is taken. A side step is sometimes called an open step.

**B**  **B**ack step (with a pivot). The pivot is done first with Torsion, so that the embrace remains. Then a back step is taken, crossing backwards, behind the standing leg, outside of the couple. This back step is sometimes called a backwards crossed step.

See also chapter 12 'Diagrams: Giro steps' and chapter 16 'Examples: Step sequences'.

Phases within a step:

These symbols are the geometric component phases of each step: Collect, Balance, Projection (including placement of foot), partial weight transfer, which then becomes full weight transfer. All these are assumed for every step and are only used if a step is only partially completed. Symbols representing component phases of a step are written in lower case, where possible.

**c**  Foot brought in towards the axis (*collect*). The extended foot is brought in to the balance point, but no weight is then put onto it (unlike the symbol #).

**ө**  Balance phase. The moment (period of time) with/of balance.

**p**  Only a **p**rojection of the foot. The movement ends with a pose: the completion of the projection phase, when the extending foot is placed. There is no subsequent weight transfer.

**∩**  Weight (axis/balance) partially transfers.

**Π**  Weight (axis/balance) completely transfers.

See also chapter 13 'Diagrams: Phases of a step', as well as chapter 19 'Musicality'.

# Rasche Notation

<u>Grammar/punctuation-for the understanding of symbols and step symbols:</u>

| | |
|---|---|
| **.** | A full stop indicates the completion of a step symbol, or a move. Only required if there are insufficient gaps between step symbols. |
| **,** | A comma is used to separate the various simultaneous parts of a movement. A move can have two 'what goes where' parts happening at the same time, described with a separating comma. |
| **(...)** | Round brackets enclose any further information, notes and described details. Bracketed information is located after the 'what goes where' step symbol. Brackets are the same as superscript: |
| Superscript | Used for further information, notes and to describe details. It is an alternative to using round brackets, so that it saves space. |
| Subscript | Subscript is used to save space. It can be used for lower priority symbols within a step symbol. The switch to/from subscript is an alternative to using a comma. |
| **Bold** | Used for highlighting important parts of the notation, such as cues, points of reference etc. |

<u>Other 'what goes where' symbols and for describing further information:</u>

| | |
|---|---|
| ‡ | The inter-axis line. From one dancer's axis to the other's axis. |
| ¥ | Embrace. This includes the whole upper body(-ies) of the couple, including the head ☺, left arm ¬ and right arm ⌐. It can also describe a lean, if it's qualified with: ¥(/) a lean, ¥ (V) away from each other, or ¥ (Λ) towards each other. |
| Φ | Axis of rotation or weight/axis/balance. Consider this as an imaginary vertical line of balance. Compare with Θ the balance phase, which is a period of time. Assume the axis of rotation is vertical. It can also be described as leaning (see above). |
| T | Torsion. The upper body rotates: the torso twists at the waist. Torsion is uniquely described with clock directions relative to the dancer's hips, as this is how a dancer will perceive it. See chapter 10 'Diagrams: Clock directions for Torsion'. |
| í, è | Breathing: in (inhale), breathe out (exhale). |
| @ | Via, to, towards, at or around to. |
| € | Leading, so as to allow the partner to do the steps as indicated. |
| Ω | Leg(s), (as opposed to foot/feet which are assumed). |
| f | Adornment (*firulete*). Can be described in brackets e.g. f(tap), or can be annotated and then described elsewhere. |
| Rpt. | Repeat (of phrase...). |
| = | Next to, against, or contact with (...what, describe in brackets). Assume contact is outside of..., otherwise use the information (%). |
| ≠ | Is not, or not the same as, or opposite to. |
| ∂ | Dynamic movement, or energy. E.g. Θ(∂) dynamic balance phase. |

Rotation symbols:
The types of rotation and turning within Tango are quite varied, and these can be described in different ways. Each step can have an element of rotation, be it of both dancers, one dancer or a part of a dancer. It is easy to over describe the rotations that take place, so the writing uses some assumptions.

With the assumption that the reader has knowledge of Tango, some rotations would be implied and need not be expressed at all; some notated steps naturally contain rotation. For example, using complex symbols S, F, $ and B the movements pass the partner, thereby rotation of the couple is already there. These rotations can be described as reactive, as they result from the steps as they are carried out. Reactive rotations can be omitted, since by describing the steps, the information is sufficient to understand the rotations.

Rotation needs to be written down if it is actively lead (proactive), or as information for clarity. Rotation can also be described in terms of 'what goes where'. This includes what rotates (inter-axis line ‡ of the couple, an individual dancer ¥, their lower body C+/C- or upper body T), the centre of rotation (@...), the direction of rotation (C+/C-), and the amount of rotation (determined with a clock direction, or indeterminate without one). The axis of rotation is assumed to be vertical (otherwise use Ø ).

Describing rotation, the following symbols are used:

‡       Using the inter-axis line symbol describes the rotation of the couple as a whole, and is written on the Description line. Used with a clock direction (to be exact), or with C+ or C-, it describes where the inter-axis line will rotate to, with the centre of rotation assumed to be the man's axis.

¥       This symbol describes the shape of the embrace. If it is written on a dance line with a clock direction, it describes that dancer's whole body rotation within the embrace. E.g. the woman turns her back to the man with ¥(6).

C+, C-       Describes a pivot where the lower body (hips and legs) turn, twisting from the waist. The pivot is clockwise or anticlockwise. The C+ and C- symbols, when in brackets, can also be used as further information, describing the direction of any rotation, without specifying its extent. Exact rotations are defined by adding clock directions.

T       Torsion: the upper body rotates, whereby the torso twists at the waist. This describes the upper body rotating away from the **hips**. Torsion is unique in that the clock direction is defined relative to the dancer's hip direction. Compare this with the symbols C+ and C- which also have a twist in the waist, but the hips rotate away from the upper body i.e. inter-axis line. See chapter 10 'Diagrams: Clock directions for Torsion'.

"Don't be afraid to take a big step if one is indicated."
David Lloyd George 1863-1945


"Is it two steps forwards, one step back;
or one step forward and two steps back?"
Linus Torvalds, inventor of Linux OS

# Diagrams and examples

## 8 Diagrams: Clock directions

Clock directions are an important abbreviation within RaNote, they can indicate any destination for a movement. They are always read as if the numbers of a clock face are written on the floor around the dancers. All of the numbers therefore, from 1 to 12, indicate a specific direction.

To read the imagined clock face, and associated directions, a few things need considering. These include where the centre of the clock is, and where the direction of 12 is. Furthermore, RaNote has assumptions about some clock directions, whereby in some cases, the number is not written but implied.

For clock directions, the following are always the case:
- When a clock direction is written down, it must always have a preceding symbol, describing what is affected.
- The clock is always in the horizontal plane (i.e. seen from above).
- The imaginary clock face is large (in other words, if the man's clock direction is 2, this is not sideways for her, but parallel). It is as if the numbers are written on the horizon.
- The centre of the clock face is as seen from the observer's axis, therefore it's according to which line it's written on.

The following is a diagram of the clock directions as the man sees them (this is also the general assumption for directions):

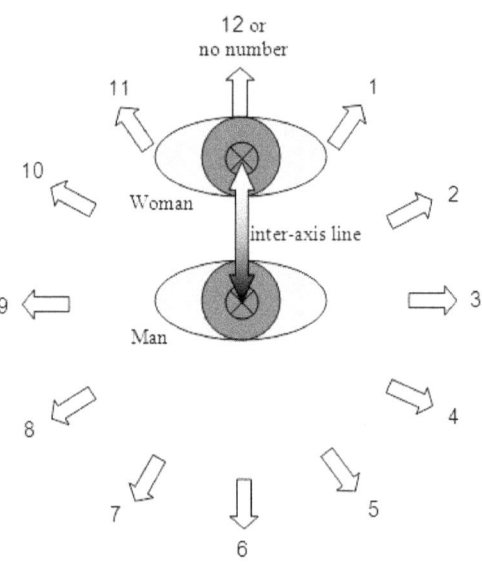

Diagrams and examples

As the woman sees it, her directions are reversed, i.e. the same as the man's, unless they are written in brackets. If no clock direction number is written, it is assumed she takes the same clock direction as the man. Her clock directions are:

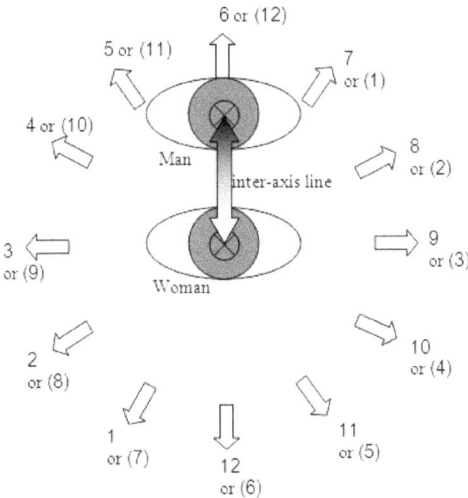

Clock directions for steps

The clock directions associated with a step are those most commonly used in RaNote. For example L3 describes the left leg stepping towards clock direction 3.

If the clock directions are in brackets and written on the Woman's W dance line, then the directions are from her perspective. The centre is her axis, and her direction 12 is along the inter-axis line, toward the man's axis.

No clock directions:

If a symbol is written without a clock direction it describes one of the following:

- Written on M line, the direction is straight ahead i.e. clock direction 12.
- Written on W line, the direction is the same direction as man's, i.e. she moves with him.
- The symbol does not need a clock direction, as a full statement of 'what goes where' is described.

Some symbols do not require a clock direction, as the destination of a step is relative to the partner. These include % and the *giro* symbols S, F, $ and B.

Special uses of symbols using clock directions are described in: chapter 9 'Diagrams: Clock directions for stage', chapter 10 'Diagrams: Clock directions for Torsion' and chapter 11 'Diagrams: Close steps'.

## 9 Diagrams: Clock directions for stage §

On stage, there are two things to consider: where the dancers are on stage, and in which direction they are facing.

The locations on stage are described as **Centre**, **Left**, **Right**, **Up** stage and **D**own stage, from the performer's perspective:

| | Audience | |
|---|---|---|
| DL | D | DR |
| L | C | R |
| UL | U | UR |

The direction the couple is facing is described as the clock direction of the audience. As previously, the clock directions are relative to the inter-axis line (assumed from the man's perspective). The following illustration shows the couple sideways to the audience, with the open side of the embrace nearest the audience. The man is on the left in this illustration, and the woman is on the right. This is described with the step symbol §9

Audience

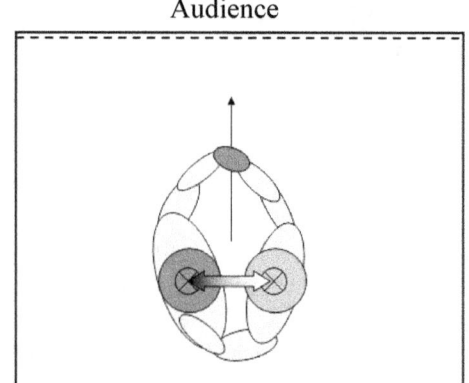

Man　　　　　　　　　　　　　　　　　　　　Woman

**§9** describes the audience to be in clock direction 9

Combining these symbols, if the couple are up stage left, with the man facing (and woman her back to) the audience, it is §UL, the same as writing §12UL . This symbol is written on the description line, as it applies to both dancers.

## 10 Diagrams: Clock directions for Torsion T

Torsion (the twist of the upper body from the waist) is the exception for clock directions, where directions are not described relative to the inter-axis line, but instead, they are described relative to the direction the dancer's hips.

The reason for this is because it is more intuitive and easier to describe the rotation of torsion, between the upper and lower body, relative to one's own hips. This is instead of trying to describe a similar position with combinations of the symbols ‡, C+, C- and ¥ with clock directions, especially as the upper body is part of the inter-axis line through the embrace and the clock direction would describe itself.

For either dancer, the following diagram shows a rectangle for the hips, and the location of the feet. The upper body is straight; this could be described with the symbol T12 or simply T since this implies direction 12, the natural position (to be straight, or to straighten up):

Shoulders/
upper body →

Hips legs

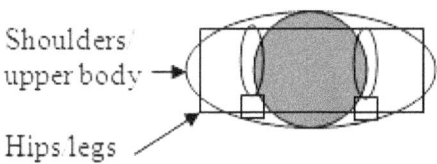

If a clock direction is described with the torsion symbol, the shoulders rotate relative to the hips. Below is an illustration of the symbol T2 whereby the hips and feet remain, but the upper body has rotated to face clock direction 2.

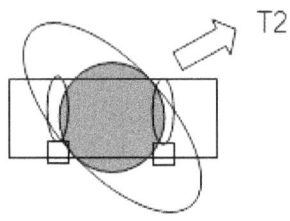

T2

## 11 Diagrams: Close steps # c

The symbols # and c are similar steps indicating that the step closes against the other foot. The difference between them is that the symbol # is a complete step, so that it is placed <u>and</u> takes weight; the symbol c however, is a *collect* only, whereby the step is incomplete, i.e. no placement and weight put onto the foot (it may be moving to another position, depending on the subsequent step symbols).

If the symbols # or c are used without a clock direction, it implies that the foot closes to its natural position next to the standing foot. Therefore, the right foot would move to the right of the standing (left) foot, or the left foot would move to the left of the standing (right) foot. See illustrations below.

The following illustrations indicate which symbol is used for the various destinations of the moving foot. Symbols without a clock direction, indicating they move to a natural position, are in bold text. The standing foot is shaded black, the moving foot is white:

L... Left foot                    R... Right foot

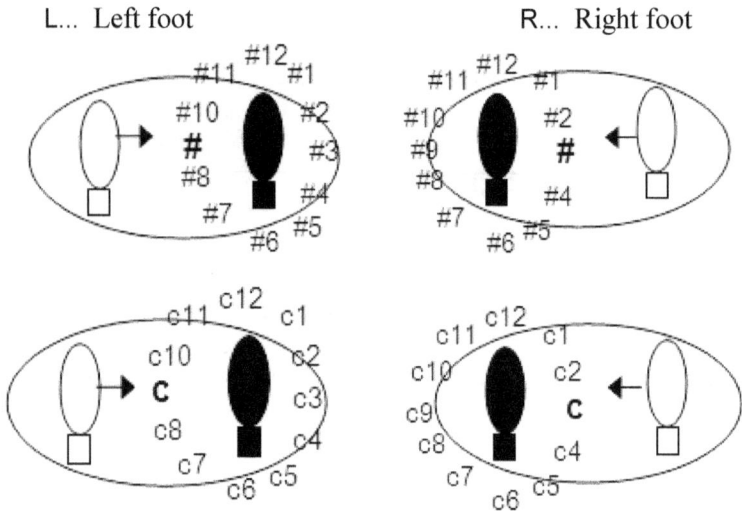

For example, for the woman's cross step (*cruzada*), her left foot steps to be next to the (standing) right foot, with the little toes touching, written on her dance line as L#(3) (brackets describe clock directions from her perspective).

Traditional foot positions (used in ballet and other dances) can be described:

| | | | |
|---|---|---|---|
| First | Lc | Rc | |
| Second | L9p | R3p | Note: these describe the position of |
| Third | Lc10 | Rc2 | the feet, but not the directions that |
| Fourth | L12p | R12p | the feet are pointing. |
| Fifth | Lc11 | Rc11 | |

46

## 12 Diagrams: Giro steps S F $ B

The *giro* steps are complex steps, containing more than one movement and describing the placement of steps relative to the partner, rather than relative to a clock direction. The *giro* steps, as described with symbols S, F, $ and B are used to describe the placement on an imaginary circle around the partner:

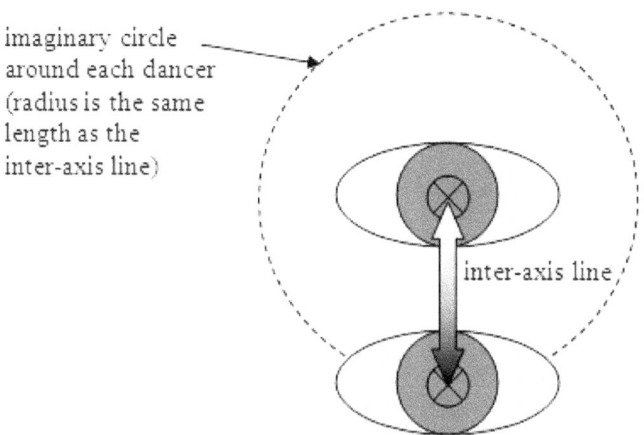

imaginary circle around each dancer (radius is the same length as the inter-axis line)

inter-axis line

The size of this circle is the natural distance to step around the partner, which is the same as the separating distance of the embrace.

If the S, F, $ and B symbols are used, but notated with an underline, this changes the step length. However, this is not in a straight line; a solid underline indicates a step further round onto the circle, and a dotted underline will indicate a shorter step, also on the circle.

The symbols S, F, $ and B are the same for the man and woman. Both are equal in the couple, and each dancer is dancing around the other.

Within a step, the point of reference is the axis of the other dancer. Their axis may be stationary, or it may move, as they take their step. If the partner is moving, then the placement of the foot will need to take this into consideration, so that it will be located on the circle at the end of the step. A dancer with knowledge of Tango will understand this.

The S, F, $ and B symbols are an extremely useful way to describe steps of each dancer within the couple, as they describe movements relative to, and around their partner, unlike the clock directions, which describe directions in a more absolute and static way.

Illustrating the free foot that moves (shaded clear), the foot can move to its new position either via within the couple (i.e. within the circle, in front of the dancer), or outside of the couple (i.e. round the back of the dancer). The dashed lines suggest the origins of the steps.

When standing on the right foot, the left foot can move either to the left (as a side step), or to the right (either as a forwards or back step). These diagrams indicate the possibilities:

Left foot to the left            Left foot to the right

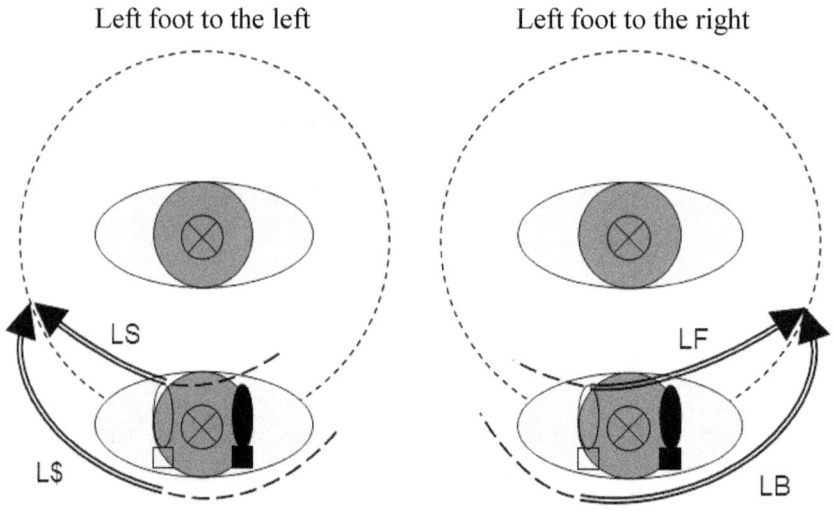

The shaded black footprints are the standing feet (the right feet).
The left feet are moving in the direction of the arrows, originating from somewhere along the arrows/dashed lines.

Notice in diagram 'Left foot to the left' that the left foot movement marked with LS travels on the inside of the standing foot (within the circle), whereas the L$ travels via the outside of the standing foot (beyond the circle).

Notice also that in the diagram 'Left foot to the right' that the left foot movement marked with LF travels on the inside of the standing foot (within the circle), whereas the LB travels via the outside of the standing foot (beyond the circle).

The $ and B steps go via the outside of the standing foot. It is clear that these steps go further and are therefore longer. They also have a pivot around the standing foot (the extent depends also on the origin of the moving foot).

The S and F steps are shorter and are linear (they do not require the pivot). For choreography, it is useful to note that a shorter step takes less time, whereas a longer step takes more.

When standing on the left foot, the right foot can move either to the right (as a side step), or to the left (either as a forwards or back step). These following diagrams indicate the possibilities.

The shaded black footprints are the standing feet (there are two left feet). The right feet are moving in the direction of the arrows and originating from somewhere along the arrows/dotted lines.

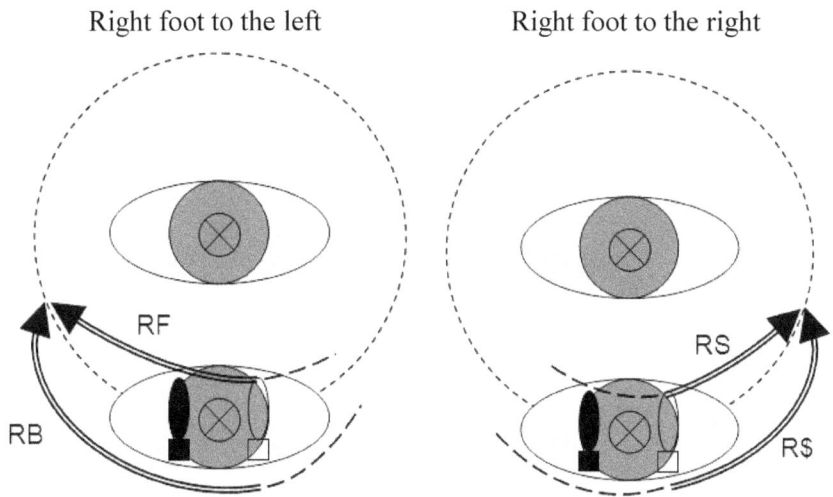

Right foot to the left                         Right foot to the right

Notice in the diagram 'Right foot to the left' that the right foot movement marked with RF travels on the inside of the standing foot (within the circle), whereas the RB travels via the outside of the standing foot (beyond the circle).

Notice also that in the diagram 'Right foot to the right' that the right foot movement marked with RS travels on the inside of the standing foot (within the circle), whereas the R$ travels via the outside of the standing foot (beyond the circle).

A *giro* has the four types of steps: side S, forwards F, side $ (with pivot) and back B (with pivot) in sequence. If the *giro* rotates:

Clockwise C+ *giro*, the left foot takes side steps:     LS    RF    L$    RB...
Anticlockwise C- *giro*, the right takes side steps:    RS    LF    R$    LB...

It is clear that when doing a *giro*, there is no swapping of the feet in the sequence, without the direction of rotation changing.

The following diagram shows the *giro* step sequence, starting with the right foot (shaded white/clear) forwards, into a clockwise *giro* (left foot is black). Note that an anticlockwise *giro* is exactly the same but mirrored:

| Sequence: | **1** | **2** | **3** | **4** | ... (repeat) ... |
|---|---|---|---|---|---|
| RaNote step symbols: | **RF** | **L$** | **RB** | **LS** | ... |
| | | | | | |
| Inside or outside step: | in | out | out | in | ... |
| Lower body pivots: | c- | C+ | C+ | c- | ... |
| Resulting Torsion: | T2 | T | T10 | T | ... |
| Standing (pivoting) leg: | (ΦL) | (ΦR) | (ΦL) | (ΦR) | ... |
| Crossed or open step: | crossed | open | crossed | open | ... |

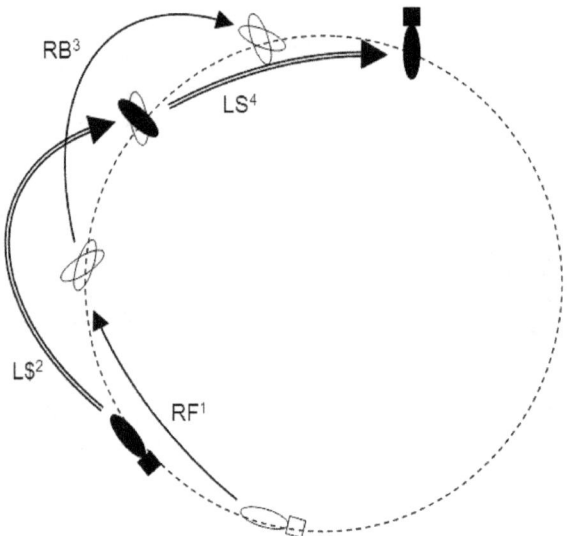

A *giro* is often taught with a continuous movement around a chair, as if dancing around a partner. The above illustration has opened the sequence out for clarity, which would otherwise be rather more confusing to look at:

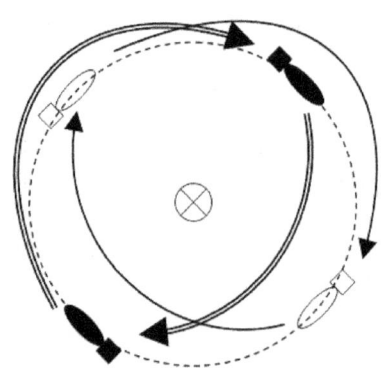

# Diagrams and examples

## Open and crossed steps

Depending on different teaching methods, the *giro* steps are sometimes referred to as either open or crossed steps. This method describes the giro steps in terms of the three destinations that these steps have:

1) F forwards crossed step: the free foot crosses in front of the standing foot.
2) B backwards crossed step: the free foot crosses behind the standing foot.
3) S or $ are both side open step(s): the free foot opens to the side.

In RaNote however, the *giro* steps are described with four symbols. Both the side steps S and $ have the same destination, hence the basis for both symbols is an S. Using both step symbols helps to distinguish whether the step originates as an inside side step S (crossing in front of the standing foot) or an external side step $ (with a pivot). This also matches the four steps of a *giro* sequence, as well as enabling better choreography. An inside side step S is a linear, short and therefore quick step. An external side step has further to travel, has a pivot and therefore takes longer to do.

Due to the differences of whether the step is taken from the inside S or outside $ of the standing leg, certain figures will become possible. For example, after a partner's step between feet %, the side step now has different options to negotiate the leg, depending if it's an S or $. A *sacada* (displacement) works for the steps around the outside, i.e. for the outside side step $ (and B). For the inside steps S (and F) this will result in, for example, a *gancho* (hook step), a *barrida* (a barrier, where the foot is pushed) or a step over (↑) the foot that's in the way. This is useful for a choreographer to know.

An alternative method to illustrate the four *giro* steps (in terms of direction of movement, not destination), for either foot is:

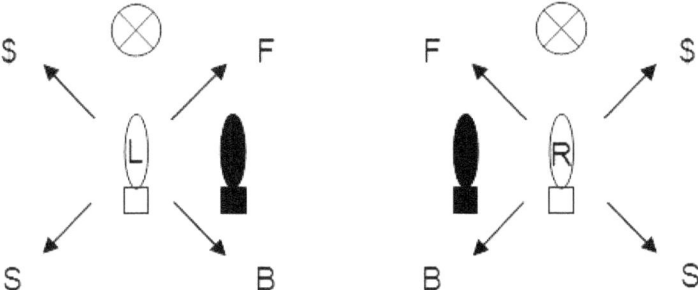

Remember: the destination of a *giro* step is <u>always</u> assumed to be onto the partner's circle (it is easy to misinterpret the above diagrams). Therefore, for the above to work, the dancers will be moving to accommodate this, or they twist or pivot sufficiently. To describe steps away from the partner (not placed onto the partner's circle) e.g. a side step back away from the partner (sometimes confusingly called an 'open back step'), the *giro* steps are not appropriate, so clock directions are a better way to describe this (e.g. MR4 ).

## 13 Diagrams: Phases of a step  c Θ p ∩ ⊓

RaNote describes the movements in Tango by using step symbols to describe snap shots of successive destination geometries. In other words, each step symbol describes the final destination of every movement. The dance is smooth, so we assume the fluid movement from one snap shot to another. Furthermore, subtle accommodating movements (e.g. changes in the embrace) are also assumed. If steps do not flow fluidly into one another, in particular if a step is not fully completed, then we need to be able to describe the sub components, i.e. the phases of steps in more detail.

The following diagram illustrates the phases within a step and at what point which step symbol represents the step. This is related to the music (the Compás count). Note that the feet are shaded differently for clarity e.g. the left foot is black, the right white/clear.

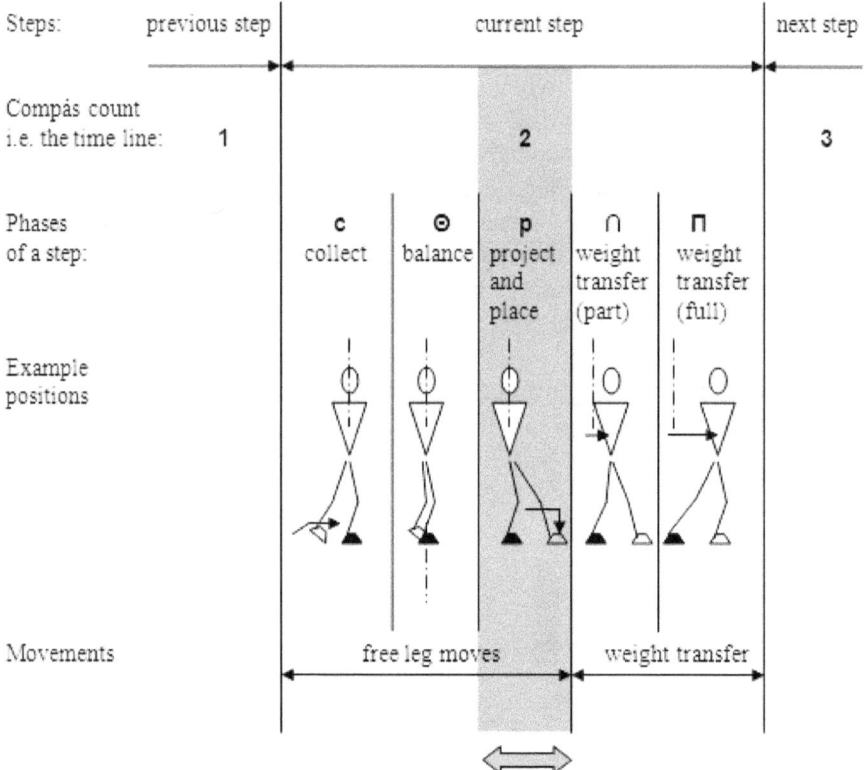

For each step, the foot placement (destination) is described with a step symbol. This coincides with the Compás count.

## 14 Examples: Step symbols

This chapter looks at examples of RaNote step symbols, together with explanations of what they describe.

**L**        This symbol is written without a clock direction. Therefore, using the assumptions: if it is written on the man's M dance line, it describes his left foot moving forwards, or if it's written on the woman's W dance line, it describes her left foot moving in the same direction that the man is going (mirroring him).

**L10**      Written on the man's dance line, this symbol describes the left foot moving to his left forward side. If it's written on the woman's dance line, it describes her left foot moving back and to her right. For her, it is the same as L(4)

**L2**       Written on the man's M dance line, this describes the left foot stepping in clock direction 2 to his right side. Written on the woman's W dance line, it is a back left step with the left, or L(8)

**L(4)**     This symbol can also be written $L^4$ where superscript is the same as writing something in brackets.

**L(9)**     Written on the woman's dance line, this describes her left side step. This is in clock direction 3, but written from her perspective (she's facing the opposite direction to him). It can also be written $L^9$ because superscript can be used as an alternative to brackets.

**L̲**        A bigger or longer (left) step is underlined with a continuous line. If it is underlined with a dotted underline L̲ it describes a smaller step. Note the general observation that with continuous movement, faster steps are smaller steps, and conversely slower steps are bigger.

**LF...RF...**  For writing *ochos* (literally eights), they can be explained in the description line with W8+ and W8- describing the woman's forward and backward *ocho* movements. However, within the dance lines, numbers indicate a clock direction, and can therefore be confusing. Furthermore, an *ocho* is a description of a movement rather than a destination, so, using RaNote, we would describe just the consecutive destinations. A forwards *ocho* would therefore be described with repeats of F , and conversely repeats of B for back *ochos*. So LF  RF  LF... describes forwards *ochos* and  RB  LB  RB... describes back *ochos*.

**C+**     If this symbol is written on either the M or W dance lines, it describes a clockwise pivot (from the waist down). If it is written on the description line, the couple rotates (i.e. the inter-axis line rotates), with the centre of rotation not defined (it's implied by the steps that are taken).

**C+2**    With a clock direction, the destination of the rotation is specified.

**C+(ΦL)**  Describes a clockwise pivot, with information in brackets that it's on (or over) the left foot. This can also be written $C+^{\Phi L}$

**cC+**    Describes the free leg collected, i.e. brought to the balance point, first, followed by a clockwise pivot. That a leg collects is normally assumed, but can be specified for better understanding.
The symbols C+ and C- can be confused with the *collect* phase symbol c. To understand which is which, the rotations always have a + or − sign and the C is written in capitals. Also, the C+ and C- are often extra information, which means they are in brackets, or alternatively elevated into superscript, after the symbol. In contrast, the *collect* symbol c is usually written at the start of a step symbol, in lower case and without a + or − sign.

**C+,ПL**  This step symbol describes a clockwise pivot, which, as it proceeds, the balance point moves to be completely on the left. The comma separates the various parts of one movement. This can also be written $C+_{\Pi L}$ whereby the change to subscript replaces the need for a comma, as well as saving space.

**(C+)**   If enclosed in brackets, the symbol describes further information (a clockwise rotation), without a specified destination.

**€(C-)**  If written on M man's dance line, it describes a lead, so as to enable the woman's step. The lead is anticlockwise.

**Φ(/)**   Describes the axis or balance towards the partner (a lean), which will in turn be supported. The balance (what) has no direction indicated, hence the assumption is forwards towards the partner (goes where). This is used for *volcada* steps.

**Φ(/≠M)** On the W line, this describes a lean back away from the man, e.g. for *colgada* steps. Specifically, it describes a lean that is not towards the man. It can also be written $\Phi^{/\neq M}$. It could also be written Φ(V) or ¥(V) to be easier to read.

54

**#**  Describes the free leg steps to the closed position, where weight is transferred onto it. The context describes which foot it is (based on the assumption of steps taken with alternate feet), otherwise it is labelled e.g. L# or R#. See chapter 11: Diagrams: Close steps.

**#12**  Describes (for the man) his free leg stepping directly in front of, and touching, the standing foot. Direction 12 needs to be specified for this, because no direction (as above) would describe the neutral position, i.e. next to the standing leg.

**L#(3)**  Describes (for the woman) the cross step (*cruzada*), where her left leg steps to the outside of the right (standing) foot, with little toes touching. It can be written $L\#^3$

**L(=R)**  Written on the man's dance line, this describes the left leg steps forwards with contact (=) to the woman's (assumed) right (R) outside (assumed) foot (assumed). This can be reduced to $L^{=R}$. To describe the contact with the inside foot, use L(=%R).

**L%**  Written on the Man's line: L% means that his left foot (what) is placed between the her feet (goes where). It suggests that his left foot is placed to enable the subsequent steps, or else to be half way between the woman's feet. Specific locations for the placement of the step can be described, for example, L% if the left foot is placed with a larger step between the partner's feet. Alternatively, a description can follow in brackets e.g. L%(@WR) or $L\%^{@WR}$ the man's left foot is placed between the woman's feet, towards her right foot, or L%(=R) or $L\%^{=R}$ with contact to the right foot. However, with knowledge of Tango, the exact position is clear, depending on the subsequent steps.

A time delay for the man is implied, whereby the partner moves first, as the geometry of these steps would otherwise not be possible. In other words, it is a reduction of the step symbol L%? Also, if this is not the case, writing the step symbol L%! indicates an early placement of left foot between the partner's feet.

The symbol % is often used with steps such as a displacement (*sacada*). *Sacadas* are possible with outside *giro* steps $ and B. If % is used for inside steps S or F, it will likely require a hook step (*gancho*), or a push out of the way (*barrida*) or similar.

**L%(=LΩ)**  Written on the man's dance line, this describes the left leg steps forwards between her legs (%), with contact (=) to the woman's (assumed) left (L) leg (Ω). This can be reduced in size to $L\%^{=L\Omega}$. Step symbols of this length can often be avoided, as the context (prior and especially subsequent steps) suggest information, so perhaps just L% or even L% are good alternatives.

**cL**      Describes a *collect* first, then a left foot forwards (i.e. direction 12 if on the M line). It is an abbreviation of Lc.L12 which describes two 'what goes where' movements. If Lc were written, it only describes the left foot collects; if context implies that the left moves, then only c is needed to describe the left foot collects.

**$_{c3}$LS**      Describes a left side step. As part of the step, first there is a *firulete* (an embellishment) within the movement, which is the left foot collects (moving towards the balance foot without weight placed onto it) to position 3, before the side step. In other words, for the man, the left foot moves to cross over the right and then moves on to become a side step. It could be written fLS (the firulete's not specified), or if the left foot is implied fS. The minor part of the step is subscripted, reducing its size and importance; it makes the step symbol easier to read. In terms of musical timing, the side step is placed on the beat that's written above it in the Compás line. With the use of subscript, this saves space and suggests the presence of a grammatical mark: a comma.

**R∩**      Using the syntax 'what goes where', this describes the right foot taking a step forwards and weight partly transferred. A forward step is assumed (written on the M line), because there is no clock direction (it is a reduction of the step symbol R12∩ ).

**∩R**      As opposed to the above, ∩R means that the weight (what) is partly transferred onto the right foot (the right foot doesn't move). The symbol ∩ shows the weight (what) is partly transferred onto the right foot R (goes where).

**RT2**      Describes a forwards step with the right foot, together with a twist in the waist so that upper body turns to the right, facing clock direction 2. This is a condensed version of R12,T2 whereby no number assumes straight ahead (on the M line), and a comma is unnecessary because each of the symbols is understood to be a complete statement of 'what goes where'.

**RSp**      Describes the right foot (what) to the side (goes where), but the step ends with the projecting phase, i.e. the foot is placed but without subsequent weight transfer. The projection phase has no subsequent weight transfer onto the right foot.

**RF(↑)**      Describes a right forwards giro step with a step over (the obstacle, i.e. the partner's foot). The right forwards step is the end destination. If however, the step symbol R↑ is used, this describes the end destination of a high right kick.

**S**    A side step is only in one direction, and depends on which foot one stands. Standing on the left foot, only the right foot can go out, and standing on the right foot, only the left foot can go out. If context implies which leg will move, then LS or RS is not needed. Since S is a *giro* step, it describes the placement of a step relative to the partner, making this a very useful symbol.

**T**    Describes the body straightening up, i.e. torsion is resolved (No Torsion clock direction means the natural position, or i.e. clock direction 12, relative to the dancer's hips). It is a condensed version of T12.

**#T**    Describes the free leg closing against the other, and the body straightening up, i.e. torsion is resolved. It is a condensed version (context makes it clear the left leg moves) of L#,T12. A comma becomes unnecessary because each of the symbols is understood to be a complete statement of 'what goes where'. The symbol could also be written T# but since steps are used to mark time (comparing them to the Compás line), it's better to describe these first. If the step symbol is written T!# torsion is resolved early, though this may be too much information for a dancer who knows Tango. It could also be written #$_T$ indicating the principle movement as the close. It is at the discretion of the writer.

**T2>**    Describes torsion, maintained for a time, until there is a resolving symbol, or with a later > symbol. The resolving symbols include T, ¥, % and the complex symbols that contain torsion S, F, $ and B. The context of subsequent steps will define this.

**¥3**    Written on a dance line, it describes a change in the dancer's embrace so that the whole dancer rotates to face clock direction 3.

**¥(open)**    Written on the Description line, the symbol describes the embrace (for both dancers) to be open. It can also be written ¥$^{open}$

**‡C+**    Written on the Description line, the couple (i.e. the inter-axis line) rotates clockwise. It can also be written ‡$_{C+}$ . An alternative is to write C+ on the Description line, and since this will apply to the whole couple, it will also describe them rotating clockwise.

**c**    Describes a *collect* only, closing of the foot to the natural position, but it is not a step, as there is no subsequent weight put onto it (otherwise the symbol # would be used). The suggestion is that the context makes it clear which foot is free, and therefore to which foot this symbol applies.

## 15 Examples: Walking geometries

This chapter looks at the various walking geometries, and how these are described using RaNote. These geometries describe the alignment of the two dancers, and which feet move when they both take a step together.

### Walking (ordinary)

For the man to walk straight forwards, starting with the man's left foot, and the woman following with her right, it is written:

| C | | | | |
|---|---|---|---|---|
| D | | | | |
| M | L | R | L | R |
| W | R | L | R | L |

Normal walking has the opposite feet moving together, meaning that when the man's left leg goes forwards, the woman's right goes back, and vice versa. There are three geometries when walking like this:

I) Walking, the man and woman are directly in front of each other. This is as illustrated above.

II) Walking, each dancer has their partner on their right side. The man's right leg, when stepping forward, passes to the left (outside) of the woman's right (standing) leg. Walking type (II) is written:

| C | | | | | |
|---|---|---|---|---|---|
| D | | | | | |
| M | L | RF | L | RF | |
| W | R | L | R | L | |

Note: since we assume the feet alternate, the right foot is implied, so RF can be F

Both dancers walk in the same direction (parallel). Like a railway, they follow two offset, but parallel, lines.

III) Walking, each dancer has their partner on their left side. The man's left leg, when stepping forward, passes the right (outside) of the woman's left and (standing) leg. Walking type (III) is written:

| C | | | | |
|---|---|---|---|---|
| D | | | | |
| M | LF | R | LF | R |
| W | R | L | R | L |

## Crossed walking

Crossed walking is out of synchronisation, in other words the same feet of both dancers move together. When the man's right foot goes forwards, the woman's right foot goes back, and vice versa. Crossed walking has two geometries:

IV) Walking, the man is aligned to the left of the woman. The man's right leg steps forwards, in line with the woman's right leg which steps back. His right leg passes the inside of her left leg. Walking type (IV) is written:

| C | | | | |
|---|---|---|---|---|
| D | | | | |
| M | L | RF | L | RF |
| W | L | R | L | R |

V) Walking, the man is aligned to the right of the woman. The man's left leg steps forwards, in line with the woman's left leg which steps back. His right left is to the right of her right leg. Walking type (V) is written:

| C | | | | |
|---|---|---|---|---|
| D | | | | |
| M | LF | R | LF | R |
| W | L | R | L | R |

All of these walking geometries require some accommodating Torsion, or twist in the waist, to a greater or lesser degree. This is because the shape of the embrace is maintained, but which is also inherently asymmetrical (it has an open and a closed side). Therefore, keeping the embrace, but walking in a parallel direction, requires some accommodating Torsion. The most comfortable walking geometries, i.e. those which compliment the shape of the embrace with the least twist, are the most commonly danced. These are geometries I, II and IV.

The use of F is the same as saying that some of these steps are best described as *giro* steps, rather than steps with a clock direction. The *giro* steps describe the placement position relative to the partner, which more accurately describes what is going on. There is no need to try to describe the embrace shapes, steps and passing positions separately. Using the *giro* forwards step F, a forwards step crossing the partner is described in its entirety.

Normally, *giro* steps are understood to have a circular movement. However, by accommodating the fact that the dancers want to move in a straight, it is as if the circular movement is opened out, the dancers adjusting their Torsion accordingly. The steps between the F steps will also have Torsion, aligning the dancers so that they remain next to each other throughout, keeping the shape of embrace.

## 16 Examples: Step sequences

This chapter looks at examples of step sequences, and how they can be described with RaNote.

## La Base

An example of a simple step sequence of repeated steps is *La base* (base):

| C | 1 | 2 | 3 | 4 | 5 | 6 | |
|---|---|---|---|---|---|---|---|
| D | | | | | | | ... |
| M | R6 | LS | RF | L | RS | L6 | Rpt. |
| W | L | R | L | R | L | RF | Rpt. |

## Basic Step

The following is the eight-count Basic Step (*paso basico*). Variations of it exist, taught by different teachers, but this is sufficient to illustrate how it might be described using RaNote. *Salida* (to 'lead out' when starting) and *Resolution* describe component step combinations in the Basic Step.

| C | 1 | 2 | 3 | 4 | 5 | 6 | 7 | 8 |
|---|---|---|---|---|---|---|---|---|
| D | | {Salida | | | }X | {Resolution | | } |
| M | R6 | LS | RF | L | T# | L | RS | # |
| W | L | R | L | R | #(3) | R | L | # |

Step 1 is sometimes taught with just a weight change (to prevent a step backwards into the unknown):

| C | 1 |
|---|---|
| D | |
| M | ⊓R |
| W | ⊓L |

The *Resolution* consists of steps 6,7,8 (RS or R3 are similar).

| C | 6 | 7 | 8 |
|---|---|---|---|
| D | Resolution | | |
| M | L | R3 | # |
| W | R | L | # |

The starting position is not normally described, and is assumed to be such that the first step(s) becomes possible. For example, if the first step moves the left foot, the starting position will be with the weight on the right and the feet closed. This starting position is called the home position.

The man's step LS (his left leg takes a big step to the side) can also be written as LS,T2 but this is not necessary: experienced dancers of Tango understand that a bigger side step will require an element of torsion to keep the embrace with the woman (also, that she would reciprocate with torsion). The *giro* symbols contain torsion, of which S is one.

The woman's left step #(3) means the woman's left leg closes i.e. is placed next to the standing (right) leg at position 3 (the legs are crossed, with little toes touching). This is the cross step (*cruzada*), and labelled X.

## Variations on the Basic Step in the cross system

The *salida cruzada* is a step combination that uses the cross system of walking, so that by count 3 the walking is in the crossed system. In this first variation, the man uses a double step at count 2 to change into the cross system, and then reverts back by taking a step over two counts (5 and 6). It can be written:

| C | 1 | 2 | | 3 | 4 | 5 | 6 | 7 | 8 |
|---|---|---|---|---|---|---|---|---|---|
| D | | | | | | X | {Resolution | | } |
| M | R6 | LS | # | L | RF | Lc.T | L | RS | # |
| W | L | R | | L | R | #(3) | R | L | # |

The step on count 1 is described as a back step, but refer to the comment in the Basic Step about it just being a weight change.

An alternative step combination to the above, [named *caminada* (literally: to walk) by my teachers Fredi Gutzler & Leila El-Jarad] is if the man takes only one step between counts 2 and 3, thereby changing between the normal and crossed system. It then reverts as above over two counts (5 and 6):

| C | 1 | 2 | 3 | 4 | 5 | 6 | 7 | 8 |
|---|---|---|---|---|---|---|---|---|
| D | | | | | X | {Resolution | | } |
| M | R6 | LS | ‡(C-) | R? | Lc.T | L | RS | # |
| W | L | R | LB | R | #(3) | R | L | # |

The delay in the man's step at count 4, marked with ? indicates that he follows her movement; his foot does not overtake her foot.

## Cambio de Frente

This is an anticlockwise C- rotation step combination, while progressing along in a straight direction. Notice that the last step (count 9) is the same as the step on 3 in the *caminada* above; so the step concludes in the same way.

| C | 1 | 2 | 3 | 4 | 5 | 6 | 7 | 8 | 9 |
|---|---|---|---|---|---|---|---|---|---|
| D | | | | < C- | | | | | > ... |
| M | R6 | LS | RF | L1 | R$ | LB | RS | LS | ‡(C-) |
| W | L | R | L | R | LS | RF | L(12) | R$ | LB |

## Ocho

There are two types of steps called *ochos*, literally eights. These are the *Ocho adelante*, the forwards ocho, where the free foot moves toe first around the standing foot, and the *Ocho atrás*, the backwards ocho, where the free foot moves heel first around the standing foot. They are described below relative to the basic step. Note, for reference, the departure points from the basic step are also marked (the previous Basic Step Compás counts with $^{bas}$). The step $^{bas}5$ is the cross step, also labelled X above.

The woman's *Ocho adelante* the forwards ocho, from basic step count 5:

| C | 1 | and | 2 | and | 3 | and | 4 |
|---|---|-----|---|-----|---|-----|---|
| D | $^{bas}5$ | f-ocho | | f-ocho | | | $^{bas}6...$ |
| M | R# | € | T3 | € | € | T | L |
| W | L#(3) | C- | RF | C+ | LF | Rc | R |

Note that the man can lead the ochos without taking any steps, so only his lead is described. The step symbol Rc describes the right leg collects. The pivots of the forwards ochos have been labelled f-ocho.

The woman's *Ocho atrás*, the backwards ocho. This can be written to fit to 8 musical counts:

| C | 1 | & | 2 | 3 | 4 | 5 | 6 | 7 | 8 |
|---|---|---|---|---|---|---|---|---|---|
| D | $^{bas}2$ | | | b-ocho | | b-ocho | | follow | $^{bas}5...$ |
| M | LS | # | LS | c€ | RS | c€ | L | R? | # |
| W | R | C- | LB | C+ | RB | C- | LB | R | #(3) |

The step symbol c€ shows a *collect* phase of the free leg, as well as a lead to enable the woman's step. Pivots of the backwards ochos are labelled b-ocho.

## Cut ocho

The *ocho cortado*, or cut ocho, is a step sequence that fits the shortest of musical sections, typically half of a phrase: four Compás counts:

| C | 1 | & | 2 | 3 | & | 4 |
|---|---|---|---|---|---|---|
| D | { | | | | | } |
| M | Lp | ⊓R | # | RSp | ⊓L | #€ |
| W | Rp | ⊓L | # | Lp | ⊓R | #(3) |

# Diagrams and examples

## Giro

The steps in a turn have been described earlier as the *giro* steps S, F, $ and B. These are the steps taken by each dancer, as they go around in a circular movement around their partner. These are usually danced in this sequence, which then repeats. A *giro* may start and end with any of these steps.

Since the *giro* steps are in a sequence, they become very useful step symbols to use when describing a step sequence (a combination of steps and moves into a figure). This is especially the case, because either dancer can dance the *giro* steps. See also chapter 7 'The <u>M</u>an and <u>W</u>oman dance lines – step symbols' and chapter 12 'Diagrams: Giro steps' for more information.

The following step sequence is particular in that it describes a *giro* turn, using *giro* steps, and which also has numbers given to the various geometries in the turn (which are used by some teachers). It is called *giro con sacadas*, as it includes displacements (*sacadas*) ; seen with the steps between the partners' legs %. This makes it useful as an example to describe here. The numbers associated with the geometries are count positions, and continue from the counts of the Basic Step as described earlier. The step starts from a slight variation of the Basic Step count 5, whereby the man tucks his right foot behind the left MR#7. The numbers of the positions are indicated in bold on the Description line. Note that these are descriptions of step geometries, not steps to music, so the Compás line has no counts:

|  | | | | | | | | | | |
|---|---|---|---|---|---|---|---|---|---|---|
| C | - | - | - | - | & | - | - | - | - | - |
| D | **$^{bas}$5** X | **6** C+ | **7** | **8** | **9** | **10** | **11** | **12** | b-ocho... | |
| M | R#7 | L% | R% | LS | $f^{Rtap}$ | R% | L% | RS | c€ | ... |
| W | L#(3) | RF | L$ | RB | S | RF | L$ | RB | C- | ... |

The rotation is clockwise, which starts with the woman's right foot at the count 6, doing a forwards crossed step. She can only go clockwise, when doing a forwards cross step with the right foot. To see how the step sequence ends, compare the position marked b-ocho with the backwards ocho previously described at the Compás count 5.

Alternatively, the ending can be with a forwards ocho. Note the Description line numbers are different: they count the 8 steps of this *giro con sacada*:

|  | | | | | | | | | | | |
|---|---|---|---|---|---|---|---|---|---|---|---|
| C | - | - | - | - | & | - | - | - | & | - | - |
| D | | **1** C+ | **2** | **3** | **4** | **5** | **6** | **7** | | **8** | ... |
| M | R#7 | L% | R% | LS | $f^{Rtap}$ | R% | L% | RF | c | L$ | R# ... |
| W | L#(3) | RF | L$ | RB | S | RF | L$ | RB. | LS. | RF | LF.T... |

The step ends with the *resolution*, as described previously in the Basic Step (*paso basico*) steps 6, 7 and 8. This *giro* can also rotate anticlockwise C-, whereby it only needs the feet to be swapped for counts 1 to 8, and the start and finish steps need to be chosen according to the different geometries.

## 17 Example: Full transcription of a Tango

Music: Recuerdo by Osvaldo Pugliese.

**A1**

| C  A1 | 1 | 2 | 3 | 4 | 5 | 6 | 7 | 8 |
|---|---|---|---|---|---|---|---|---|
| D §9 Start from a pose | | | | | start of movement | | | |
| M  LSp | - | - | - | - | c | > | > | |
| W  RSp | - | - | - | - | c | > | > | |

**A2**

| C  A2 | 1 | & | 2 | & | 3 | & | 4 | & | 5 | & | 6 | & | 7 | & | 8 |
|---|---|---|---|---|---|---|---|---|---|---|---|---|---|---|---|
| D | | | | | | | {*C+ | 5L5 | sacada | | | | | | } |
| M | L6p c | | L6p | L6 | R# | ΠL | L | R% | > | | € | | ΠL | | R6  L#3 |
| W | L(6)p c | | L(6)p.c | | ΠL | R | L | | RB | | c(3) | | LS | | RF  c |

**A3**

| C  A3 | 1 | 2 | 3 | 4 | 5 | 6 | 7 | 8 |
|---|---|---|---|---|---|---|---|---|
| D | {11  5R5 | | - | - | - | } | - {Resolution | } |
| M | R6 | L9 | cf | R | L= | # | L=  RS | # |
| W | - | LS | R# | L | R(6) | #(3) | R(6)  LS | # |

**A4**

| C  A4 | a | 1 | & | 2 | & | 3 | 4 | 5 | 6 | 7 |
|---|---|---|---|---|---|---|---|---|---|---|
| D | | {C+  4R4 | | | | 3 | | {C+  5R5 | | } |
| M | - | - | RF | L$ | L$ | R4 | RF | L$ (5 melody) | L (6 melody) | L (7 melody)  R  c4 |
| W | - | - | L | R | LS | LS | L | R# | R | L  c(9) |

64

**C B1**

| | 1 | 2 | 3 | 4 | 5 | 6 | 7 | 8 |
|---|---|---|---|---|---|---|---|---|
| D | §3 | | | {C+ Wgiro | | | | {Wochos+ |
| M | L6∩ | ∩R | RFp | ΦΠR^C- | (planeo) | L%=p | ¿ | ∏L |
| W | R  c | # L | R# | R$  LF | LB  RS | LF | Φ^C- | RF↑  Φ^C+ |

**C B2**

| | 1 | 2 | 3 | 4 | 5 | 6 | 7 | 8 |
|---|---|---|---|---|---|---|---|---|
| D | | ¿ | | skip | | | {10 3R5 Wochos+ | |
| M | RF | Lc | L9p | ΦLtoR∏R | LF | R3p | RF | LS |
| W | LF | T,R# | L(9)p | ΦLtoR∏R | LF | R# | L | RS  LF |

**C B3**

| | 1 | 2 | 3 | 4 | 5 | 6 | 7 | 8 |
|---|---|---|---|---|---|---|---|---|
| D | | ¿ | ¿ | {10 5L5 | | | | ¿ |
| M | € | € | R# | L | R6 | LS | RF | L$ |
| W | RF | € | c | R | L | RS | L | R#.T |
| | | RF | LF | | | | | |

**C B4**

| | 1 | 2 | 3 | 4 | 5 | - | 7 | - |
|---|---|---|---|---|---|---|---|---|
| D | boleos | | | | | | | |
| M | Rf | RF | € | € | Lf^planeo | - | Lc | |
| W | Lf^boleo | LF | R$ | LB | RS | | LF | |

**C A₂1   1**
D Rpt.B1
⇨

| | 1 | 2 | 3 | 4 | 5 | 6 | 7 | 8 |
|---|---|---|---|---|---|---|---|---|
| M | | | | | | | | |
| W | | | | | | | | |

**C A₂2**
D Rpt. row B2
⇨
M
W

**C A₂3**
D Rpt. row B3
⇨
M
W

**C A₂4   1 & 2   3   -   5   6   7   -**
D Rpt. row B4
⇨
M
W

65

| C C1 | 1 | 2 | 3 | 4 | 5 | 6 | | 7 | 8 |
|---|---|---|---|---|---|---|---|---|---|
| D | §9. ¥(as start).... | | | > | | | | ∫8 6R4 | 8 |
| M | LSp | > | > | > | L# | R | L# | R6 | LS R# |
| W | RSp | > | > | > | R# | L | R# | L | RS R# |

| C C2 | 1 | 2 | 3 | 4 | 5 | 6 | 7 | 8 |
|---|---|---|---|---|---|---|---|---|
| D | | feet touch | | ∫ ʃ RF | bicycleta | | | 8 ∫ |
| M | LS | Rp= | RB | L#. | LB=f@ | > | R6∩ | ∏L |
| W | LB | RB | - | - | Lf@ | > | L | RF |

| C C3 | 1 | 2 | 3 | 4 | 5 | 6 | 7 | 8 |
|---|---|---|---|---|---|---|---|---|
| D | ∫Wf | | | | | | ∫ | *Rpt of** ∫C+ 5L5 |
| M | € | > | > | > | > | > | R# | L |
| W | C+.Lf front | | C-(4) | L | C+(2).L@ high kick | | L#(3) | R |

| C C4 | 1 | 2 | 3 | 4 | 5 | 6 | 7 | 8 |
|---|---|---|---|---|---|---|---|---|
| D | sacada | | | | ∫ | ∫6R 3:3 | - | ∫ |
| M | R% | > | € | ∏L | R6 | L#3 | R6 | L#3 | R6 |
| W | L(7) | RB | c(3) | LS | RF | c | L | R | L |

### C A₃1

| | 1 | - | 3 | - | 5 | - | 7 | - |
|---|---|---|---|---|---|---|---|---|
| D | {11 7L7 | | | | | | | |
| M | LS | R | R | | f^back f^front | f^front f^back | f^front | f^front |
| W | R | L | L | | f^front f^back | f^back f^front | f^back | f^back |

### C A₃2

| | 1 | - | 3 | - | 5 | - | 7 | - |
|---|---|---|---|---|---|---|---|---|
| D | | | | | {7 5R6 } | | | |
| M | R | L | RS | L | # | R6 | L6 | R6 |
| W | L | R | L | R | # | L | RF | L |

### C A₃3

| | 1 | - | 3 | - | 5 | 6 | 7 | 8 |
|---|---|---|---|---|---|---|---|---|
| D | { | { | gancho. voleo | | gancho } | | | |
| M | LS | RF | Lc^tap | LS | R% € L$ | RF | LB=↑ | f^gan . R6p |
| W | R | L | # | LB | RB L^gan L^vol | LBp | L(%) | RFp? |

### C A₃4

| | 1 | & | 2 | & | 3 | & | 4 | & | 5 | & | 6 | & | 7 | & | 8 |
|---|---|---|---|---|---|---|---|---|---|---|---|---|---|---|---|
| D | {**C+ 2L7 | | C+(ΦL) | | some ganchos.... | | | | | } | | | | | |
| M | Rf^gan .RB | LS | | RFp | Rf^gan | RB | RB | Lf^gan | LS | LB | RB | Lf^gan | R%∩.L$ | LB | RF∩ |
| W | | RF | | LF | R%p | R#^C+ | R#^C+ | L%p | L%p | LB | RB | Lf^gan | LB | | RB∩ |

### C A₃5

| | 1 | & | 2 | & | 3 | & | 4 | & | 5 | & | 6 | & | 7 | & |
|---|---|---|---|---|---|---|---|---|---|---|---|---|---|---|
| D | {C+ 2L7 (Rpt of**) | | | | C+(ΦL) | | | | | | | §3 } §. | | Smile. End |
| M | R8∩ | Rf^gan | | | RB | | RFp | | Rf^gan | RB | RB | Lf^gan | LS∩ | € |
| W | RFp↑ | | | | LS | | LS | | R%∩ | R#^C+ | | L%p | RF | ¥^C- |

"Knowledge advances by steps, and not by leaps"
Baron Macaulay (Thomas Babington) 1800-1859


"Ultimately the best way to understand a highly
changed situation is to take a step back"
Peter Greenaway

.

# Using RaNote

**18 How to write, transcribe and choreograph using RaNote**
You can write RaNote steps following this step-by-step guide to take you through your thought processes and decisions. The aim is to create clear, legible and simple to understand notation. You can compare the steps with the process diagram for writing a step symbol at the end of this chapter. This uses the same principles for writing step symbols as described in Chapter 3: 'Understanding RaNote – it's easy!', which are:

- Use symbols to reduce the amount of writing (abbreviate key words)
- Use the syntax rule 'what goes where'
- Use assumptions
- Notate unusual elements
- Remove the obvious
- Place the step symbols into the dance lines, to the music.

1) Writing begins with a set of blank RaNote staves.[1]
This can be done on the computer, by hand or by using pre-printed pages. The recommended computer font is Arial 10 point. Usually, each music phrase corresponds to one row of a RaNote stave, stretching across the page. Pre-printed pages are available as Rasche Notation Notebooks.[1]

2) Once the RaNote stave is created, the music form needs to be identified, so that the Compás line can receive the Phrase labels. Then, the Compás count, to refer the timing of steps, is needed. This is the simple time count, and is typically eight counts per phrase. The number of regular Compás counts per phrase will be repeated throughout the piece. Therefore, once established, the Compás count can be copied onto all the staves.

3) Listen to the music, and edit the Compás count, according to what is audible. By recognising if the music is in simple, half or double time. Cross out the inaudible beats (replace with - ) for half time, and add & or a for the in-between beats of double time. Edit any other rhythmical elements.

4) Write in any key bits of information into the Description line.

5) Each movement, or, to be exact, the destination of each movement is described with each step symbol. First, the man's movements are described with step symbols written on his dance line. Then, the woman's movements are described with step symbols on her dance line. To write a step symbol, the syntax 'what goes where' is kept in mind. First, what moves ('what...')? Principally, it is the feet (and hence legs) that move, therefore the choice is between the left L or right R symbols. See chapter 7 'The Man and Woman dance lines – step symbols' for other 'what...' symbols.

[1] See note at end of this chapter.

6) Then, whatever moves also has a destination ('...goes where'), which is its final location. This can be described relative the dancer's position (using the clock directions) or relative to the partner (by using the *giro* symbols S, F, $ or B, or % step between). See chapter 7 'The Man and Woman dance lines – step symbols' for other '...goes where' symbols.

7) The next thing to consider in the movement is whether the step is completed, or whether the step is only partially completed. A fully completed step begins with a *collect* c, then a balance point/phase ⊖, then a projection p, and then the weight is transferred onto the placed foot- partially ∩ and then fully ∏. If the step ends at one of these phases, then this is written into the step symbol, describing the destination. For example, a left side step, which ends with the projection, without subsequent weight transfer, is written LSp.

8) The step symbol has now been created, and it may need slight adjustment to convey more information. This could be that the step is big (underline the step symbol), small (dotted underline the step symbol), ahead of the partner's movement (add the symbol !) or behind the partner's movement (add the symbol ?). The dancer breathes in (í) or out (è). Within the step, there may be an adornment f (*firulete*), or if, for example within the step, the free leg moves through the closed position first, the symbol can include a *collect* cLSp. Any other information can also be added as a note in brackets after the step symbol. See chapter 7 'The Man and Woman dance lines – step symbols' for other symbols that can reduce the amount of written notes.

9) Once a step symbol is created, it often has a lot of information. It is then necessary to consider how a symbol may be reduced, using the principles and assumptions of RaNote, together with the context of the step symbol. For example, it is assumed that the dancers who read RaNote have knowledge of Tango, therefore, with the steps that are described, information about the leading need not be included: the dancers will know how to lead it. With the use of assumptions, only the exceptions to the rules are required.

10) Once the step symbol is reduced, it can be changed in its appearance to give priority to the important parts (the main part of the step). This is possible using the subscript, which reduces the symbols to a smaller size. Also, if text or symbols are put in superscript, this is equivalent to that text being in brackets. Superscript not only reduces the space of the symbols, but also negates the need for brackets. For example, the symbols representing a part of a step, for the purposes of priority, are already defined in a lower case. Subscript reduces space and lowers the priority of what's written, and can be used in place of a separating comma.

9) If the step symbols are closely packed together, or happen simultaneously, then the grammar symbols, including comma and full stops, should be used.

# Rasche Notation

## Transcribing using RaNote

A transcription using RaNote is the process of writing down steps that you see on a video of Tango. By transcribing a dance, it translates and reproduces it into a more readable and flexible format than video. The following are a few simple suggested steps to transcribe steps from a video, and are similar to those previously described:

First, start with the music. It can be broken down into its form, once the different and repeated sections are recognised. This can then be further broken down into phrases, and labelled. Then, copy the Compás counts onto every Compás line. These will repeat throughout the all the phrases, even if only some of these are accented.

Complete the Compás lines by editing the Compás counts according to the audible and accented beats. Inaudible counts become a dash, and extra audible beats receive a mark, such as & or ‘.

Put written information (cues and step names) into the Description line. Once done, the two context lines provide an excellent way of navigating through the music, identifying sections, phrases and notes within it.

Then, describe the Man's steps in detail, especially as the directions of movements all refer back to him. Once done, the Woman's steps can be described in detail.

If the steps are difficult to see in a video (e.g. too fast), here are a few hints:
Choose a particular count on the Compás line, and freeze frame there.
Each time this is done, observe one dancer only.
Observe which foot is moving.
Observe where it is placed, especially where in relation to the partner.
Observe the same moment without freeze framing it to confirm.
Repeat the above for the other dancer.
Again observe without freeze framing, and compare with the Compás line.

RaNote naturally fits this sequence of thinking. The lines are organised:

| C | First: | Write the music Compás |
|---|--------|------------------------|
| D | Second: | Describe and annotate |
| M | Third: | Detail of Man's steps |
| W | | Detail of Woman's steps |

## Choreographing using RaNote

Choreographing is a different process to transcribing. Whereas transcribing requires observation, choreographing requires creativity. It is difficult to suggest an ideal way to be creative, as it's different for different people.

There is however always a context and a starting point, from which a choreography takes shape. The context is for whom, doing what and to what ends, the choreography is intended. The actual writing of steps can begin when there is a combination of two things, the music and the vocabulary of steps and movements that are available (to both dancers). This is so, even if all the possible steps are not present in the mind: the music inspires a feeling, and in turn a step or movement will be recalled, which fits the music...

Tango, when danced in the dance halls, is an improvised dance, whereas the music is not improvised, even if it's played live. There are two types of Tango performances, either a demonstration of improvisation, or a demonstration of the dancers' ability. A choreography (or part choreography) is relevant for the latter situation, where display steps are chosen to fit to the music. As it is the case that Tango music is not improvised, it becomes possible, and more usual, to work from the music towards a choreography. The structure of RaNote lends itself well to this.

For both the music and the dance, there is one key concept applicable to both, and that is phrasing. If a piece of music has been chosen, it will already contain music phrases, and understanding this format is a good step to creating a choreography. Individual movements combine into continuous movements, and these are formed into dance phrases. RaNote lends itself well to the writing of both types of phrases. By using RaNote, the construct, symmetries and layering within a piece can be explored. For example, repetitions (of themes) are easily labelled and described, and therefore become apparent.

The defining element that makes a musical phrase is the ending, i.e. a cadence. This is comparable to a normal sentence which ends with a full stop, or a partial ending with a comma. Similarly, a dance phrase can be defined in those terms, whereby a resolution ends a phrase (complete or in part).

In the context of a stage production, there are cues to follow, or other dancers to include in the performances. The cues can easily be included as a note in the Description lines. If these are written in bold text, they will be clearly visible as points of reference. To choreograph numerous dancers together, multiple dance lines can be written below the stave. This is similar to the orchestration in music, where numerous music staves are combined together, for the various instruments.

[1]Rasche Notation Notebook

To notate dance steps using RaNote, it is simple to create the RaNote staves either on the computer or long hand on paper. An easier alternative is to use a Rasche Notation Notebook, which contains sheets with rows of staves and Compás counts pre-printed on them. They look as follows:

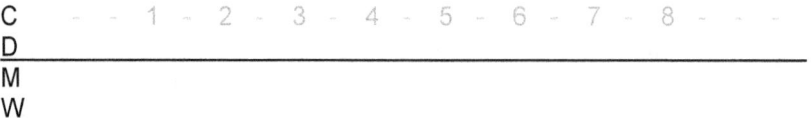

The Notebooks are in A4 size, so the spacing is more generous than shown above. The staves are evenly spaced out down the pages and grouped so that they suit the length of Tango music. The pre-printed Compás counts are evenly spaced out across each row, allowing sufficient space for extra symbols. Also, this regular spacing helps you to write your steps neatly into all the other lines of the stave, across the page.

Included in each notebook are sheets that contain sufficient rows of these staves so that a full choreography to any piece of Tango music is possible and fits well. The sheets have 8 and 12 Compás count staves, as well as some sheets with Compás counts left blank. There is even a summary of the RaNote symbols for your quick reference!

The Rasche Notation Notebooks are an excellent way to help you write down and remember your Tango steps. People who have used them have felt that they have benefitted from using the pre-printed booklet to keep their thoughts and notes neat and together.

For more information about the Rasche Notation Notebooks, and where these can be obtained, see the reference chapter 'Further information'. You can also find out more at www.RascheNotation.com

## How to write a step symbol

**Is it the Left or Right foot that moves?**
Start with the symbols:
L left or R right.

⇩

**Add a destination symbol:**
A clock direction[2], or:
S   Side step across partner.
F   Forwards step across partner.
$   Side step across partner, that has a pivot e.g. after an F step.
B   Back step across partner, that has a pivot e.g. after a $ step.
%   Step between partner's feet.
#   Destination is next to the standing foot, to a natural position.

If the step is not complete, use:
c   The moving foot moves to the natural position (next to axis), but isn't placed.
p   The moving foot projects and places, but no weight is transferred.
∩   Step ends with part weight transfer
Π   The step ends with full weight transfer

⇩

**(...)  Add information in brackets, using:**
Ω   Legs
@   Via, to, towards, at or around to
Θ   Balance phase
=   Is next to
≠   Is not the same as, or opposite to
‡   Inter-axis line
C+   Clockwise rotation direction
C-   Anticlockwise rotation direction
∂   Dynamic movement
Also, use long-hand notes or annotate.

⇩

**Adjust the movement destination**
!, ?   Ahead, or delayed step
___ : ....   Bigger or smaller step
>   Continuation of a step
<...>   Enclose one step
f   *Firulete* (adornment)

---

**If it is not a foot that moves, start with:**
C+  Lower body pivots
C-  Lower body pivots
T  Upper body rotates
‡  Inter-axis line
¥  Embrace
Φ  Weight/axis/balance

∩  Part weight transfer
Π  Full weight transfers

Other movement types:
−  No movement
€  Lead partner's step
í  Inhale
è  Exhale

For # or c, if the destination is not the natural position, also add a clock direction[2].

---

For C+/C-, T, ‡ and ¥: to specify a direction, add clock direction[2]

For Φ or ¥, lean add (in brackets) /, Λ (in) V (out)

For ∩ and Π, add a destination:
L onto left foot
R onto right foot

Use C+ or C- in brackets for turn direction info.

Go to box: 'Reduce...'

---

[2]**Note for clock directions:**
For the man:
[no number]  Ahead (clock direction 12)
1-11      Clock direction

For the woman:
[no number]  Same as Man's direction
1-12      Clock direction, as he sees it.
(1)-(12)   Relative to her, as she sees it.

---

**Reduce the information:**
See context and remove the obvious/assumed.

---

**Use grammar:**
subscript   To reduce the size of symbols.
superscript   To reduce bracketed info.
**Bold**   High-lights

---

**Align step symbol under the Compás count.**

---

**Tidy, with the use of grammar:**
.   If step symbols aren't sufficiently separated for clarity, use a full stop: completion of a step.
,   Multiple simultaneous symbols, use commas.

## 19 Musicality

This chapter looks at how various timing of steps and musicality can be written and expressed using RaNote.

### Timing of step placements

As described previously, each step is defined as beginning with a *collect* phase, then balance, projection/ placement, partial weight transfer and full weight transfer phases. The step ends with the full weight transfer (i.e. the *collect* belongs to the next step). The marking of the music occurs with the placement of the feet on the ground. This example shows some steps with the placement of the feet on the beats, Compás counts 1 to 4:

| C | 1 | 2 | 3 | 4 |
|---|---|---|---|---|
| D | | | | |
| M | L | R | L | # |
| W | R | L | R | # |

By showing the steps to be taken between the beats, the line below implies that consecutive balance points are on the beats, rather than the placement of the feet:

| C | 1 | 2 | 3 | 4 |
|---|---|---|---|---|
| D | | | | |
| M | L | R | L | # |
| W | R | L | R | # |

Note: the Compás line suggests there are no audible in-between beats, which would otherwise have been marked and or &

If it is helpful, a note in the Description line, or a symbol e.g. ♪(Θ) can help emphasise the general assumptions of a piece, that the balance phases coincide with the Compás counts.

Applying this to the *resolution* step, as described earlier in chapter 3 'Understanding RaNote - it's easy!', it can look as follows:

| C | 1 | 2 | 3 |
|---|---|---|---|
| D | Resolution | | |
| M | L | R3 | # |
| W | R | L | # |

To illustrate what is happening, the following diagram shows the step symbol offset relative to the Compás count. Compare the diagram below with the diagram in chapter 13 'Diagrams: Phases of a step'. It also shows all the phases in a step as the smooth transition of movement proceeds. The alignment of the Compás count is the shaded area, and the alignment of the step symbol is indicated with shaded arrows.

Since the step symbol (describing the destination geometry of a step) is offset relative to the Compás count, it suggests another part or phase within the movement must coincide with the Compás count. The phase that coincides with the Compás count is taken to be the balance phase. Therefore, the timing of the dancer's step is such that the balance phase is on the music.

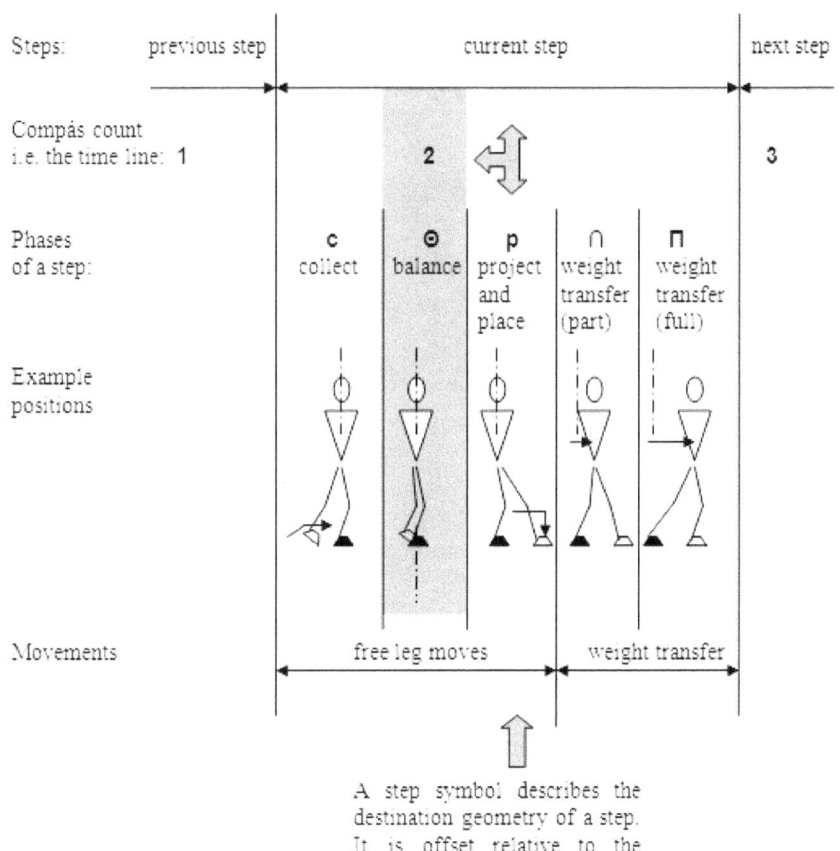

It is not possible to align the symbols in the stave for more subtle timings other than to align the count with either the placement phase or the balance phase. An example would be to dance with the start of the projection phase on the beat, as is danced in ballet. This is too detailed for the graphic alignment of step symbols beneath the Compás count, so instead, a note is required, such as ♪(end of Θ) in the Description line can best describe this.

Slurs (or articulation) marks

As described in chapter 6 'The Description Line – dance phrases and notes', a double dividing line can be used in the RaNote stave to group some Step Symbols together, into one fluid movement.

Slurs are used in music notation, written over notes, to describe them played smoothly together, so that they sound like one group of notes. They also describe the structure of phrases.

Similarly, the doubled dividing line in RaNote describes the smooth movement of steps, so that they are danced as one group of steps. They also describe the structure of the (dance) phrases.

For example, the cut ocho (*ocho cortado*), described previously, can be written with two smooth movements, as follows:

| C | 1 | & | 2 | 3 | & | 4 |
|---|---|---|---|---|---|---|
| D | | | | | | |
| M | Lp | ПR | # | RSp | ПL | #€ |
| W | Rp | ПL | # | Lp | ПR | #(3) |

Interpretation

When interpreting the music in a dance, the timing of the steps are sometimes early or ahead of the rhythm, only to catch the beats at the end of a phrase correctly (timed with the cadence). Singers use this technique to interpret the music into their own unique style. This interpretation of the music is very subtle, so it is not possible to align the symbols in the stave to show this. However, the Description line can be used to include a note about the interpretation.

The symbols ? and ! in the dance lines do not suggest the interpretation of a piece. These symbols suggest early or delayed movement in relation to the partner's step or movement, rather than to the music.

## 20 Other languages (Spanish)

RaNote can easily be used in other languages, including Spanish, since the symbols are representations of movement (destinations), rather than words.

The syntax 'what goes where' of RaNote may be less familiar in other languages, but this needs to remain constant. The symbols describing movement also remain the same. This is clear for the pictographic symbols, which are graphical representations of moves, where a translation is impossible.

For the symbols that abbreviated words however, there might be a case to argue that some symbols can change. In this regard however, the RaNote symbols were chosen for clarity, with reference to both English and Spanish languages. For example, C (Compás) originates from Spanish, and D (Description or Descripción) works in both languages. Some symbols are understandable and clear to Spanish speakers, once understood. For example, L Left (*izquierdo*) and R Right (*derecha*). If abbreviated Spanish words were used, the symbols could clash or cause confusion with other similar symbols already used.

The only alternative symbols considered for use in the Spanish version of RaNote (and will not to cause confusion if replacing the original) are:

H (*Hombre*) replacing **M** (Man) and
J (*Mujer*) replacing **W** (Woman).

| | |
|---|---|
| C | **C**ompás |
| D | **D**escripción |
| H | **H**ombre |
| J | Mu**j**er |

All the other symbols remain the same in this book.

The content of the Description line can be in any language, as it has only suggested symbols. It is there to assist with the understanding of the piece. It is the writer's choice which language he will choose to use, according to who the intended readers are.

As an academic note, the syntax of RaNote, as mentioned in chapter 3 'Understanding RaNote - it's easy!', is 'what goes where', or 'subject-action-destination'. In terms of linguistic typology, this is the Subject-Verb-Object structure which is mostly used in the English language. The Spanish language also makes significant use of the SVO structure.

## 21 Other dances

RaNote can be used for notating and choreographing other dances, other than Argentine Tango, though there are difficulties when doing so. There are assumptions made within RaNote that work for Tango, but would not be applicable, or would need to be changed, if another dance was being notated. For example, RaNote assumes prior knowledge of Argentine Tango. Also, RaNote assumes no, or very little, movement from the horizontal plane, i.e. the rise and fall of the dancers. It also does not have the vocabulary to describe movements that are unusual for Tango, such as various arm and head movements. This limits the usefulness of RaNote for other dances, and how easily it can be applied.

If the dances are broadly similar such as the movement being principally in the horizontal plane, and mostly leg movement, then there is a case for using RaNote. It would however need to be adapted for these dances.

Looking to use it elsewhere, a dance to which RaNote might be well suited to is ballroom dancing, as there are some similarities. The differences will be mostly in details and subtleties within the steps, dance and music. These will include, for example, the need to describe the movement of a toe, heel or ball of the foot. It is beyond the bounds of this book to effectively reconfigure the assumptions and symbols for the other dances, though here a few thoughts to consider, should it be required:

Some differences between Argentine Tango and Ballroom Dancing include:
-Tango has more improvisation.
-Floorcraft is more prescribed in Ballroom, where each step relates specifically to the movement in the room. Tango steps can be more adaptive.
-Ballroom has more upper body movement (swaying and head movement).
-Tango is danced more on the level, whereas Ballroom has rise and fall.
-Ballroom prescribes the use of toe, ball or heel of the foot.
-Stage versions of both types of dances break the rules, so that the partners separate, do jumps and other movements which are beyond the symbols described in this book.
-Tango has more use of Torsion, maintaining the embrace shape during steps. Ballroom has a more stable frame and posture.

In the future, if the choreography of Tango is influenced or inspired by, say, ballroom dancing, then it might be useful that the symbols that are used in those dances be adopted back into RaNote for Tango.

## Fleckerl

As an example of a Ballroom step using RaNote, a Natural (or Right) Fleckerl (pronounced Fleckle) turning clockwise can be written:

| C | 1 | 2 | 3 | 4 | 5 | 6 |
|---|---|---|---|---|---|---|
| D | | C+ | | | | |
| M | R10 | LS | R10 | LS | R8 | LS |
| W | LS | R(8) | LS | R(10) | LS | R(10) |

A Reverse (or Left) Fleckerl, turning anticlockwise can be written:

| C | 1 | 2 | 3 | 4 | 5 | 6 |
|---|---|---|---|---|---|---|
| D | | C- | | | | |
| M | L2 | RS | L2 | RS | L4 | RS |
| W | RS | L(4) | RS | L(2) | RS | L(2) |

Note, the above steps use clock directions more than the *giro* steps (S, F, $ and B) because the movements are better described this way; they are actually crosses behind or in front of the leg, without torsion.

## Fan, Flare and Ronde

Other examples of ballroom dancing steps are Fan, Flare and Ronde, where the free leg is fully extended, swinging around as the step is taken (steps $ and B). The differences are, Fan: toe brushes floor, Flare: toe above floor and Ronde: leg is elevated. Writing these in RaNote for either leg becomes:

| D | Fan | Flare | Ronde | A description can be added. |
|---|---|---|---|---|
| M or W | $@↓ | $@ | $@↑ | @ describes an extension (underlined). |

Elevation ↓ (low) ↑ (high).
Note: a Flare will normally be assumed, as it's just above the floor.

## Ballroom dancing symbols

These are some suggestions for additional symbols than can be used when describing ballroom dancing when using RaNote:

| | |
|---|---|
| ↑ or ↓ | Rise, up, lift, or Fall, down, drop. |
| Y | Sway e.g. YL is sway left. |
| ¥ | Embrace (description in brackets). |
| t, b, h | **T**oe, **B**all or **H**eel of the foot placement. Flat can be assumed. |
| ⌐ or ⌐ | Left or Right arm. |
| % | **C**ontra-body movement. |
| ☺ | Head: turn or movement. e.g. ☺ 10 is turn to the left. |
| k, fl | **K**ick: from the hip, **fl**ick: kick from the knee. (f is a *firulete*). |

Many names of steps can be written (or abbreviated) in the Description line.

"A dance to the music of time"
Anthony Powell

"That's one small step for man,
one giant leap for mankind"
Neil Armstrong

# Reference

## Glossary

| | |
|---|---|
| Axis (-rotation) | The rotational axis. See also 'Balance'. |
| Balance (-point) | The balance point, or axis. Also the Centre of Gravity. |
| Balance phase | The balance point extended (in time), due to partner interaction. For example with dynamic balance. |
| Bar | Musical bar (US: Measure). |
| Barrida (Sp.) | A push step, where a foot pushes the partner's foot along. |
| Cadence | The end of a (musical) phrase; sounds like a resolution. |
| Canción (Sp.) | Tango Canción is Tango music with singing. |
| Caminada (Sp.) | To walk. Also the name of a crossed basic step. |
| Collect (Sp.) | A phase of a step: the free leg's brought to the axis. |
| Colgada (Sp.) | A step sequence with rotation and dynamic balance. |
| Clock direction | A direction as in a clock. |
| Compás (Sp.) | The name of the top line in the stave. See Compás count. |
| Compás count | The counted regular beats per phrase. Similar throughout the piece of music, and at a stepping pace. |
| Complex step | Multiple movements represented with one step symbol. |
| Context line(s) | Two lines above the stave dividing line: C and D lines. |
| Cross step | A particular geometry of a step (WL#3), the Cruzada. |
| Crossed step | A step across (past) the partner. |
| Crossed walking | A method of walking as a couple, out of synch. |
| Cruzada (Sp.) | See Cross step. |
| Dance line(s) | Two lines below the stave dividing line: M and W lines. |
| Dance phrase | See 'Phrase'. |
| Double time | Every music beat in a bar is emphasised. A quick rhythm, double the tempo of Simple time. |
| Espejo (Sp.) | the woman follows (mirrors) the man's direction. |
| Figure | See Step Sequence. |
| Firulete (Sp.) | An adornment. |
| Follow | The interpreting of lead steps into movement. |
| Form | The major divisions of a musical piece. |
| Free leg | The leg not bearing weight, and therefore free to move. |
| Gancho (Sp.) | A hook step. |
| Giro (Sp.) | Turning steps. |
| Half time | Every first music beat in a bar is emphasised. Half the tempo of Simple time. |
| Lead | The indicating of steps to the partner. |
| Lines | Compás, Description, Man or Woman line across the page. |
| Measure | See Bar. |
| Milonga (Sp.) | Dance evening, or a type of Tango music (rhythm). |
| Movement | A complete move, incl. all associated steps, twists, etc. |
| Ocho (Sp.) | Step sequences, with forward/back pivots. |
| Phrase | A music (or dance) section, equivalent to a sentence. |
| Phrase labels | The label identifying each phrase within the music. |
| Pivot | Rotation around an axis (lower body), i.e. with Torsion. |

| Placement | A phase of a step: the placement phase. The extended foot is placed onto the ground. |
| Project | A phase of a step: the free leg extends from the axis. |
| RaNote notebook | A pre-printed booklet, containing sheets of pre-printed staves, for writing RaNote. See 'Further Information'. |
| RaNote stave | The four lines: Compás, Description, Man and Woman. |
| Resolution (Sp.) | A step sequence: resolution of a/the step. |
| Row | The four stave lines, written across the page. |
| Sacada (Sp.) | A step sequence with a displacement of a leg's movement. |
| Salida (Sp.) | A step sequence: exit (onto the floor). |
| Simple time | Every second musical beat in a bar is emphasised. This is the regular rhythm to dance to. It is Compás count tempo. |
| Stage | A stage or performance area. |
| Stave | See RaNote stave. |
| Step | See 'Step symbol'. |
| Step sequence | A combination of movements into a Figure, i.e. a set of Step symbols. Typically a phase of dance and lasting the length of a musical phrase. |
| Step symbol | A combination of Symbols to describe a 'what goes where' movement e.g. L6. Using assumptions, a Step symbol can often be condensed into one Symbol. |
| Symbol | individual symbol as written e.g. L. |
| Syntax | The construct of a Step symbol: 'what goes where'. |
| T-Clock Dir. | Clock directions when describing Torsion (relative to hip). |
| Tango | Argentine Tango: dance, music and culture. |
| Torsion (Sp.) | A twist in the waist (upper body rotates). |
| Transfer | A phase of a step: weight transfer between the feet. |
| Vals (Sp.) | Tango waltz music. |

## Summary of symbols

These are the symbols that are described in this book. For more detailed explanations, please see the original chapters in which the symbols appear.

The RaNote stave:

| | |
|---|---|
| **C** | The **C**ompás line, for music. |
| **D** | The **D**escription line, for comments and notes. |
| _____ | The dividing line: context lines above, dance lines below. |
| **M** | The dance line for the **M**an. |
| **W** | The dance line for the **W**oman. |

The Compás line symbols:

| | |
|---|---|
| **A2, A₂2** | Phrase labels, identifying each phrase within the music form. The letter indicates the section and the subscript indicates if it's a repeat. Numbers indicate the phrase within each section. |
| 1,2,3,4,5... | The regular Compás counts within a phrase. |
| \| | Indicates the end of a phrase. This is not required if the end of a phrase coincides with the end of a row. |
| - | Non-accented Compás count. |
| and, & | Half count beats (between the rhythmical counts). |
| a | Quarter count beats. |
| ' | Any other irregular (or faster) beats/counts. |
| **Bold** | Bold text, highlights a particular symbol, count or beat in the music. Phrase labels are highlighted this way. |
| Superscript | Can be used for clarity to describe extra details or notes, or in place of round brackets. |
| ½,⅓,⅛ | Fractions for indicating parts of the music (rhythm). |
| ♪ | A symbol abbreviating the Compás count. |

The Description line symbols:

| | |
|---|---|
| { ... } | Dance phrase: symbol and bracket (sometimes *italics*). With a destination, also a summary e.g. 4L3 (man 4 steps, starting with left, woman 3 steps, assume opposite right foot, unless x). |
| **Rpt.** | Repeat...(repeat row, music or dance phrases, or bracket info). |
| § | Stage symbol. With abbreviations of stage locations, if needed, incl.: Centre C, Left L, Right R, Up stage U and Down stage D. |
| Superscript | Grammar: Used for further information, notes and details. It saves space: small size and instead of enclosing in brackets. |
| Subscript | Grammar: Part of the step symbol, subscript saves space. Visually, subscript is less useful than superscript on the dance line, as using it adjusts the appearance of the dividing line. |
| _____ | Doubled dividing line groups step symbols together. |

Any descriptions, symbols and notes are suited for the Description line, even if written long-hand.

# Reference

## The symbols of the dance line(s):

### Essential symbols:

| | |
|---|---|
| **M, W** | **M**an(-'s), **W**oman(-'s), (stave labels for dance lines). **H**, **J** (Sp.). |
| **L, R** | **L**eft… (foot), **R**ight… (foot). |
| **S, F** | *Giro*: **S**ide step and **F**orward step, across the partner. |
| **$, B** | *Giro*: **$**ide step and **B**ack step (with pivots), across the partner. |
| **1** … **12** | Clock direction, as on a clock face. Relative to the inter-axis line. |
| **(1)** … **(12)** | Clock direction, relative to the inter-axis line, from the Woman's perspective (when written on her dance line). |
| **#** | Close. The free foot steps to be next to the standing foot. |
| **C+, C-** | Lower body pivots: Clockwise, Anticlockwise. |
| **T** | **T**orsion. Upper body rotates, from the hip. Clock dir. from hip. |
| **%** | Step between partner's feet (or info. inside of). |

### Quality of the step:

| | |
|---|---|
| **-** | No movement (i.e. a Freeze, the position is held). |
| **>, <** … **>** | Continuation of a step, or enclose a continuous movement. |
| **!, ?** | Movement is ahead, or delayed (relative to partner). |
| **___, :......** | Underline: taken as a longer/bigger, or shorter/smaller step. |

### Parts of a step symbols:

| | |
|---|---|
| **c, p** | Foot to axis (*collect*), or only **p**rojection of foot. |
| **∩, ∏** | Partial, or full weight (axis/balance) transfer. |
| **Θ** | Balance phase (a period of time). |

### Grammar:

| | |
|---|---|
| **. ,** | Full stop: end of a step. Comma: separates various parts in a step. |
| **(...)** | Brackets for further information, details and notes. |
| Superscript | Further information and notes. Same as enclosing in brackets. |
| Subscript | Part of the step symbol, subscript is used to save space. |
| **Bold** | For highlights, e.g. cues, points of reference etc. |

### Other symbols:

| | |
|---|---|
| **‡** | The inter-axis line. |
| **@** | Via, to, towards, at or around to. |
| **Φ** | The axis of rotation, or weight/axis/balance. Lean info: /, ∧ or ∨. |
| **=** | Next to, against, or contact with (...what, describe in brackets). |
| **≠** | Is not, or not the same as, or opposite to. |
| **€** | Leading, so as to allow the partner to do the steps as indicated. |
| **¥, Ω** | Embrace, and legs. |
| **f** | Adornment (*firulete*). |
| **í, è** | Breathing: in (**i**nhale), breathe out (**e**xhale). |
| **∂** | Dynamic movement, or energy. |
| **C+, C-** | Clockwise, Anticlockwise rotation information. |

## ASCII (hex) and Unicode (hex) codes:

Each symbol used in this book can be found, using MS-Word, from the 'Insert>Symbol' or 'Symbol>More symbols' pull-down menus or ribbon. Also, find out more about symbols, characters and ASCII from the 'Help' function. However, each character also has an associated ASCII or Unicode code, which is useful to know if the correct symbol is not easily found. To use these codes (e.g. in MS-Word) if the code is 0040, then type 0040 and then hold down the ALT key and press X. In other words type: 0040, Alt+X . You will get the symbol @.

| Symbol | ASCII | Symbol | ASCII | Symbol | Unicode (only) |
|---|---|---|---|---|---|
| A | 0041 | ( | 0028 | fl | F002 |
| B | 0042 | ) | 0029 | ♪ | 266A |
| b | 0062 | ‡ | 0087 | ≠ | 2660 |
| C | 0043 | # | 0023 | Ф | 0424 |
| c | 0063 | = | 003D | Θ | 0398 |
| D | 0044 | + | 002B | ∩ | 2229 |
| è | 00E8 | - | 002D | П | 041F (or 03A0) |
| F | 0046 | % | 0025 | Λ | 039B |
| f | 0066 | < | 003C | Ω | 03A9 |
| G | 0047 | > | 003E | ∂ | 2202 |
| H | 0048 | ! | 0021 | ↑ | 2191 |
| h | 0068 | ? | 003F | ↓ | 2193 |
| í | 00ED | _ | 005F | ↔ | 2194 |
| J | 004A | & | 0026 | ┐ | 2510 |
| k | 006B | \| | 007C | ┌ | 250C |
| L | 004C | @ | 0040 | ‰ | 2105 |
| l | 006C | / | 002F | ☺ | 263A |
| M | 004D | , | 002C | ● | 25CF |
| p | 0070 | . | 002E | ⅓ | 2153 |
| R | 0052 | 1 | 0031 | ⅞ | 215E |
| S | 0053 | 2 | 0032 | | |
| T | 0054 | 3 | 0033 | | |
| t | 0074 | 4 | 0034 | | |
| U | 0055 | 5 | 0035 | | |
| V | 0056 | 6 | 0036 | | |
| v | 0076 | 7 | 0037 | | |
| W | 0057 | 8 | 0038 | | |
| X | 0058 | 9 | 0039 | | |
| Y | 0059 | 0 | 0030 | Fractions can also be created | |
| $ | 0024 | § | 00A7 | by writing them e.g. 2/3. Then, | |
| € | 0080 | ½ | 00BD | convert the 2 into superscript | |
| ¥ | 0085 | \ | 005C | and 3 into subscript, to get $^2/_3$. | |

**Further information**

Official websites for Rasche Notation:
**www.RascheNotation.com**
as well as www.TangoLinks.co.uk

These websites provide all the current information, updates, links, and discussions about Rasche Notation. The website www.RascheNotation.com has the official and current information about Rasche Notation, including discussions, news, updates, developments and more.

Rasche Notation Notebook:
As described at the end of chapter 18 'How to write, transcribe and choreograph using RaNote', there are Notebooks available that contain sheets with blank RaNote staves, which are ideal for writing down choreographies, transcriptions and generally to remember your Tango steps.

Each notebook is in A4 format and contains pre-printed sheets with staves and Compás counts, making it very easy to clearly and neatly write down and transcribe all types of Tango music and steps. The size of the sheets allows for plenty of space for the Compás count and the writing of step symbols. The notebooks also contain a summary of the symbols in RaNote, for your quick reference!

Rasche Notation Notebooks are available from: **www.RascheNotation.com**
Purchasing, printing and distribution through Lulu.com

Also by Thomas Rasche:
'Argentine Tango - Class Companion' is a book that was written to accompany the teaching of Tango. Tango is more than a dance, it is also a culture; in this book, the history, context, music, dance styles, key insights and more are described, giving a wider picture of Tango. It is essential for all students of Tango, at all levels of ability.

Argentine Tango - Class Companion
The guide for students of Argentine Tango
Thomas Rasche
Published by: Lulu, 1997
ISBN 978 1 84753 532 0

Available from: **www.RascheNotation.com** and from all good bookshops.

## Further reading:

*Music theory:*
The AB guide to music theory, Part 1
Eric Taylor
Published by: The Associated Board of the Royal Schools of Music
ISBN 1 85472 446 0

Music Theory for Dummies
Michael Pilhofer, MM and Holly Day
Published by: Wiley, 2007
ISBN 978 0 7645 7838 0

*Tango music theory:*
Tango - Let's dance to the music!
Tango music for dancers without musical education
[book + DVD]
Joaquín Amenábar
Published by: Joaquín Amenábar, 2009
ISBN 978 987 05 5574 2
www.joaquinamenabar.com.ar

*Notation systems:*
Tango: The Structure of the Dance
By Mauricio Castro, Castro Mauricio, Truco Daniel
Published by Gotan Enterprises Inc, 2000
ISBN 978 9 50526 129 1

Tango: The Structure of the Dance Vol 2
By Mauricio Castro
Published by Autores Editores, 2003
ISBN 978 9 87434 598 1

El tango, una danza: Sistema Dinzel de notación coreográfica
By Rodolfo Dinzel, Gloria Dinzel
Published by Corregidor, 1997
ISBN 978 9 50051 005 9

See www.TangoLinks.co.uk (or Google search) for web links to more notation systems, including: Benesh notation, Bodirsky notation, Castro, Dinzel notation, Klement, Laban notation, Tangotation etc.

With internet search engines, try search terms such as 'tango notation', 'dance notation', 'movement notation', 'choreography' and 'kinetography'. Using translate and search options can also provide useful results.

*Tango books:*
Argentine Tango - Class Companion
The guide for students of Argentine Tango
By Thomas Rasche
Published by: Lulu, 1997
ISBN 978 1 84753 532 0

Tango: Poetry of Buenos Aires
By Horacio Salas
Published by: A. Asppan S.L., 2000
ISBN 978-9875090385

The Golden Age of Tango: An Illustrated Compendium of Its History
By Horacio Ferrer
Published by: A. Asppan S.L., 2000
ISBN 978-9509517707

Gotta Tango
By Alberto Paz and Valorie Hart
Published by: Human Kinetics, 2007
ISBN 978-0-7360-5630-4

Tango Dimensionen (in German)
By Nicole Nau
Published by: Kastell Verlag
ISBN 3-924592-65-9

Tango
Simon Collier, Artemis Cooper, Maria Susana Azzi, Richard Martin
Published by: Thames & Hudson Ltd; New edition edition, 1997
ISBN 978-0500279793

The Meaning of Tango: The Story of the Argentinian Dance
Christine Denniston
Published by: Anova, 2007
ISBN 978-1906032166

El Tango, Una Danza:
ESA Ansiosa Busqueda de La Libertad
By Rodolfo Dinzel
Published by: Corregidor, 1996
ISBN-13: 978-9500507936

**Rasche Notation developments**

There are some differences between the Rasche Notation described in this book compared to the original version described in the book 'Argentine Tango – Class Companion'. Mostly, the differences are a development of the original, however, there are a few changes that have been made, and these are worth mentioning:

- The stave, and the lines within it, are now clearly defined and (re)named.
- Clock directions are now relative to the inter-axis line ‡, the line between both dancer's axis (one exception is for Torsion).
- Assumptions are now used.
- There are extra categories of symbols, including phases within a step, and complex symbols describing and replacing multiple symbols/movements.
- The symbols ∩ and ∏ (partial and full weight transfer) are swapped.
- Geometric walking positions are not labelled i or o to be in/out of sync.
- The symbol > now describes continuous movement.
- The symbol ⊖ now describes the balance phase (time).
- The symbol ¥ now describes the shape of the embrace.
- The symbol § describes the stage (orientation and location).
- The symbol þ is no longer used.
- The symbols S and $, describing side steps, are kept as they were. Sometimes, these steps are described as open steps, so the alternative would be to replace the symbols with O and Ø respectively. This is still possible, but, for consistency, they symbols S and $, are used throughout this book.

Further developments of Rasche Notation are posted on the website www.RascheNotation.com, which will be updated with any current items.

If you would like to share your thoughts and comments, you can contact Thomas at thomas@RascheNotation.com, or you can go to the website www.RascheNotation.com and follow the links to the discussion forum.

Reference

## About the author

Thomas Rasche started dancing Argentine Tango in Berlin in 1997. From 2000 until 2006 Thomas lived and taught in Ireland. He has taught classes on behalf of Dublin Argentine Tango Society (DATS) and other promoters in Dublin, as well as in Cork and Waterford. In 2003 Thomas set up a Tango group in Mullingar, which had close links to the Longford-Westmeath Argentine Society. Since moving to the UK in 2006, he set up the Tango Lincs group in Lincolnshire, as well as having taught at the Tango Mango events in Totnes, UK. He now lives in Bristol, UK.

Thomas published the book 'Argentine Tango - Class Companion' in 2007 as a guide for students of Tango; a book that covers the history, context and information about the dance, beyond that which is taught in classes.

Thomas has done numerous performances, including "The Tango Spell" with the Pasodos dance company. He has been taught by international dancers: Damián Esell & Nancy Louzán, Jorge Firpo & Aurora Lúbiz, Osvaldo Zotto & Lorena Ermocida, Fredi Gutzler & Leila El-Jarad, Claudio Omar & María Verónica, Gabriel Angió & Natalia Games, Pablo Veron, Mariano "Chicho" Frúmboli & Eugenia Parilla, Fabián Salas & Carolina del Rivero, Rodolfo 'el Chino' Aguerrodi & Miho Omaki, Matias Facio & Kara Wenham, Ricardo Klapwijk & Nicole Nau, "El Pibe" Palermo, Ricardo Oria & Jenny Frances and more. The understanding of music by Joaquín Amenábar and others.

Thomas' dance style is of the Salons in Buenos Aires, and is characterised with smooth movement of the embracing couple across the floor. He teaches Tango in a way that enables you to quickly join a Milonga, the social dance evenings of Tango, with confidence. Tango is a fun and social dance; important are communication between the dancers in the embrace, good leading that is clear and accurate, musicality and the improvisation with steps, music and floorcraft.

Thomas can be contacted at:     Thomas@RascheNotation.com
Or visit his website at:     www.RascheNotation.com

# Index

C
D
M
W

C
D
M
W

C
D
M
W

C
D
M
W

C
D
M
W

C
D
M
W

C
D
M
W

C
D
M
W

Reference

C
D
M
W

C
D
M
W

C
D
M
W

C
D
M
W

C
D
M
W

C
D
M
W

C
D
M
W

C
D
M
W

C
D
M
W

C
D
M
W

C
D
M
W

C
D
M
W

C
D
M
W

C
D
M
W

C
D
M
W

C
D
M
W

C
D
M
W

C
D
M
W

C
D
M
W

C
D
M
W

C
D
M
W

C
D
M
W

C
D
M
W

C
D
M
W

**Also available**

To accompany this book about Rasche Notation, you can also obtain the notebooks, designed to help you write your Tango steps:

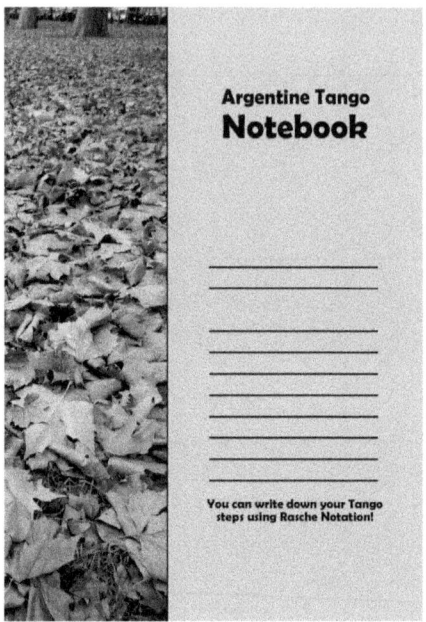

The Notebooks are in A4 size and are available with different covers.

The pages contain staves, evenly spaced out down the pages (similar to the previous few pages) and grouped so that they suit the length of Tango music. There are pre-printed Compás counts evenly spaced out across each row, allowing sufficient space for symbols. The sheets contain 8 or 12 Compás count staves, as well as some blank ones. There is even a summary of the RaNote symbols for your quick reference!

The Rasche Notation Notebooks are an excellent way to help you write down and remember your Tango steps. People who have used them have benefitted from using the pre-printed booklets to keep their thoughts and notes neat and together.

To obtain Rasche Notation Notebooks, they are exclusively available from:
www.RascheNotation.com

Previously published by Thomas Rasche is the book:
'Argentine Tango – Class Companion', ISBN 978-1-84753-532-0.
This book is also available at www.RascheNotation.com and from bookshops.

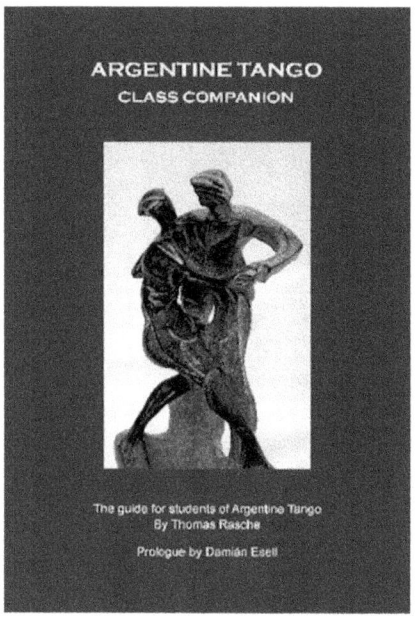

This book is written as a companion book for students taking Argentine Tango classes. In a class, you learn a step, but there is so much more to Tango: it is a culture, a history and more. This book introduces the history, culture music and more, together with underlying theory of the dance. An excellent companion to your classes!

---

You can find out more about Rasche Notation, links, discussions, and more from the website: **www.RascheNotation.com.**

www.ingramcontent.com/pod-product-compliance
Lightning Source LLC
Chambersburg PA
CBHW072226170526
45158CB00002BA/764